RESOURCE
BOOKS FOR
TEACHERS

series editor

ALAN MALEY

ART AND CRAFTS
WITH CHILDREN

Andrew Wright

OXFORD
UNIVERSITY PRESS

OXFORD
UNIVERSITY PRESS

Great Clarendon Street, Oxford OX2 6DP

Oxford University Press is a department of the University
of Oxford. It furthers the University's objective of excellence
in research, scholarship, and education by publishing
worldwide in

Oxford NewYork

Athens Auckland Bangkok Bogotá Buenos Aires
Cape Town Chennai Dar es Salaam Delhi Florence
Hong Kong Istanbul Karachi Kalcutta Kuala Lumpur
Madrid Melbourne Mexico City Mumbai Nairobi
Paris São Paulo Shanghai Singapore Taipei Tokyo
Toronto Warsaw

and associated companies in Berlin Ibadan

Oxford and *Oxford English* are registered trade marks of
Oxford University Press in the UK and in certain other countries

© Oxford University Press 2001

The moral rights of the author have been asserted

Database right Oxford University Press (maker)

First published 2001

All rights reserved. No part of this publication may be
reproduced, stored in a retrieval system, or transmitted, in any
form or by any means, without the prior permission in writing
of Oxford University Press, or as expressly permitted by law
or under terms agreed with the appropriate reprographics
rights organization. Enquiries concerning reproduction outside
the scope of the above should be sent to the ELT Rights
Department, Oxford University Press, at the address above

You must not circulate this book in any other binding or cover
and you must impose this same condition on any acquirer

Photocopying

The Publisher grants permission for the photocopying of those
pages marked 'photocopiable' according to the following
conditions. Individual purchasers may make copies for their
own use or for use by classes that they teach. School purchasers
may make copies for use by staff and students, but this
permission does not extend to additional schools or branches.

Under no circumstances may any part of this book be
photocopied for resale.

ISBN 0 19 437825 X

Printed in Hong Kong

Acknowledgements

I would like to thank:

Julia Sallabank and Alan Maley for their sensitive and thoughtful guidance in the planning and writing of this book.

The teachers and children who have tried out the activities in this book, and helped me to improve them.

Livia Farago for sharing her ideas.

My wife, Julia, for her support and professional sharing.

My children, Timea and Alexandra, for their ideas, and for their constant willingness to try out my ideas.

Line illustrations by Andrew Wright © Oxford University Press.

The publisher would like to thank the following for their permission to reproduce photographs:

The Bridgeman Art Library pp 11 (Rembrandt self portrait/ Mauritshuis, The Hague), 56 (Facsimile of Codex Atlanticus/Private Collection).

Every effort has been made to trace the owners of copyright material in this book, but we should be pleased to hear from any copyright holder whom we have been unable to contact. We apologize for any apparent negligence. If notified, the publisher will be pleased to rectify any errors or omissions at the earliest opportunity.

To Timea and Alexandra Wright

Contents

The author and series editor

Andrew Wright was a student at the Slade School of Fine Art, the premier postgraduate art school in Britain. He has continued to paint, draw, and illustrate his own books. At the same time, he has continued to work with children—both his own, and those he meets in schools, drawing, designing, making books, and producing shadow theatre productions. As an art teacher he was, for 15 years, Principle Lecturer in Art and Design at the Metropolitan University of Manchester. As an author of language teachers' resource books, he has published two other books in this series: *Storytelling with Children* and *Creating Stories with Children*. As a storyteller, story-maker, and book-maker, in the last eight years he has worked in ten countries with over 40,000 children. As a language teacher trainer he has worked in 30 countries, and was the founder of the IATEFL Young Learners Special Interest Group.

Alan Maley worked for The British Council from 1962 to 1988, serving as English Language Officer in Yugoslavia, Ghana, Italy, France, and China, and as Regional Representative in South India (Madras). From 1988 to 1993 he was Director-General of the Bell Educational Trust, Cambridge. From 1993 to 1998 he was Senior Fellow in the Department of English Language and Literature of the National University of Singapore. He is currently a freelance consultant and Director of the graduate programme at Assumption University, Bangkok. Among his publications are *Literature*, in this series, *Beyond Words*, *Sounds Interesting*, *Sounds Intriguing*, *Words*, *Variations on a Theme*, and *Drama Techniques in Language Learning* (all with Alan Duff), *The Mind's Eye* (with Françoise Grellet and Alan Duff), *Learning to Listen* and *Poem into Poem* (with Sandra Moulding), *Short and Sweet*, and *The English Teacher's Voice*. He is also Series Editor for the Oxford Supplementary Skills series.

Foreword

There was a time when teaching English to young children was conceived of as mainly a matter of involving them in songs and games. Songs and games of course remain important for young learners, but our ideas have evolved considerably in recent years. We have come to realise that, for these kinds of learners, there is a need for more than just teaching the language—rather the language is just one element in a process of helping them to develop as 'whole persons': an educational rather than just a training process.

This book is one response to this need. The focus is on involving children simultaneously in activities promoting their personal development and in helping them to learn the language. Art and craft activities serve these twin aims in an ideal fashion. While making things, the children also make meaning. As they explore shapes, colours, textures, constructions, they are extending their experience and understanding of the world—and doing it through the medium of the foreign language.

We are fortunate that, in Andrew Wright, we have a unique blend of experience and expertise in art and in language teaching. For fifteen years Andrew was a teacher of art and design. He has been able to draw on this experience to inform his later work in language teaching. As an artist, he has a proper understanding of the educational value of art and craft in developing children's understanding and sensitivity. He is passionately concerned that we should not trivialise art and craft activities just because the learners are young! As a language teacher and author, he appreciates the need to structure activities and to provide a framework of encouragement and support.

The book is a treasure house of imaginative, involving, and above all, practical activities. It is an invaluable addition to the resources of anyone involved in teaching younger learners.

Alan Maley

Introduction

Language learning and art, crafts, and design

Children learn by doing. When they are involved in art, crafts, and design activities, language can play a key part. Although much of what is done in art, crafts, and design is non-verbal, for this book I have chosen activities in which language plays a central role.

The important role of language in art, crafts, and design is evident when children are:

- listening to, and perhaps reading instructions on how to do something. They are associating the new language directly with objects, actions, and experiences, rather than merely with existing experience through translation of the mother tongue.
- making use of their existing language skills (which they employ when reading in their mother tongue), for example, when guessing meaning from context
- receiving and giving praise and encouragement
- describing, evaluating, and expressing feelings and ideas.

This range of purposes and associated language is not found in traditional foreign language teaching at primary level, in which songs, rhymes, and games are the sole diet. However good this traditional 'food' of songs and games is, it cannot provide the balanced diet essential for a child's broad conceptual development.

The value of art, crafts, and design at the lower proficiency levels

Art, crafts, and design are particularly important at the lower levels because they make a child's limited range of language part of something bigger—something which is strong, rich, and has material presence. For example, the word 'me' on its own is worth little or nothing, but written below a self-portrait of a child it becomes meaningful, and is much more likely to be remembered.

The educational value of art, crafts, and design

When working with children, we are first of all teachers who are responsible for the overall development of those in our care. Our role is to introduce activities, materials, and values which deepen their awareness and understanding of the world around them, and their relationship with it.

In my opinion, it is not enough for me merely to help the children to name a colour in English. I should also help them to become aware of the wonderful varieties of colour which we can perceive and make, and to deepen their associations with colour.

Art, crafts, and design activities can help children to:
- appreciate the world around them
- be more aware of the five senses, and develop skill in using them
- develop skill in comparing, contrasting, classifying, sequencing, and organizing
- acquire awareness of artistic form (shape, colour, line, texture, length, weight, movement, etc.) and materials, and skill in handling them. They will also become aware of the concepts represented, and their value. (Consider the value of fresh personal vision based on direct and honest response to experience, as opposed to the commonplace, the stereotype, and the cliché. As an example, think of the immense range of colours found in the bark of a tree, and contrast this with the 'pass-me-down' colour brown routinely used by children in a million pictures.)
- understand 'cause and effect', and develop a skill in discovering them
- develop a skill in problem-solving
- have a positive attitude to exploring, and to making sense of experience
- have a positive attitude to themselves, and to others, and to working with others.

Art is not just a hobby, it is a fundamental aspect of human behaviour which involves intellectual as well as emotional exploration, expression, and communication.

Who is this book for?

1 Children

This book is for use with children aged between four and twelve, and includes activities for the whole of this age range.

Clearly, there is a big difference between four- and twelve-year-olds! Very young children:
- are in the early stages of awareness of texts, whereas older children are usually fluent readers
- tend to respond to individual happenings rather than considering general principles
- are less likely to be interested in adult subject matter and perceptions than older children
- are more likely to need constant adult guidance

- are less able to sustain concentration and a sense of direction than older children
- have less manual dexterity.

Each child (like each adult) is an individual, with their own natural speed and focus of development. Some children of four can use a pair of scissors with great dexterity, for instance, while others can't. I have tended to place the age at which an activity can be done as the age when children are likely to get some satisfaction out of doing the activity, rather than the age at which they can do it easily.

Most of the activities can be adapted for use with children of different ages and at different stages of personal development.

Proficiency level
Most of the activities in this book are possible for beginners and/or elementary learners of English. Children who are more proficient in English will enjoy doing the activities at a richer linguistic level.

I firmly believe that, from the very earliest days of learning a second or foreign language, children should experience the new language through activities which are meaningful and important to them.

2   Teachers

This book is for teachers who believe that it is vital for the children to experience the new language as an important tool to be used in meaningful and enjoyable activities.

But I'm not an art and crafts teacher!
Most of the activities require no more skill than is needed to make a cup of coffee, or boil an egg. Clearly, you have to get involved in physical activity, but no previous skill and no unusual artistic talent are expected. It is not so much a personal artistic skill in the teacher which is required, but an openness to what art is and can be (see pages 11–12).

But there is already too little time for English!
Surely it is better to spend time letting the children become familiar with the language than to race them through a language marathon in which *you* finish the course but most of the children are nowhere to be seen!

If the activities engage the children, and if they really *experience* the language, the quality of learning will out-balance the time spent on the art and crafts activities.

Suggestion: Why not try to combine some art and crafts lesson time with English lesson time? It is widely accepted that primary education should be cross-curricular (see page 9).

But the mess!
Only some of the activities lead to a mess, and even these are not on the level of a pottery class, or an oil-painting class, in which all the children are working with full tins of paint and brushes in every hand. In any case, the act of cleaning up in art and crafts is very much part of the discipline of the subject, and a wonderful opportunity for 'language in use'! However, I do understand that a messy classroom could be a problem for some teachers, so I have made reference to this aspect in each of the activities where it is relevant. See also the Appendix (page 136) for suggestions on reducing mess.

But I haven't got the materials!
Few specialist materials are required in these activities.

It means more preparation time!
Many of the activities will require you to prepare for them to a certain extent. However, you will be compensated by the motivation of the children!

But we have the coursebook. Isn't that enough?
While it is true that a good coursebook will provide you and the children with a balanced diet of language experience, you might decide that the children need some extra practice in a particular area, or that they might like to embark on a creative project of their own. This is when the activities in this book can help.

Writing and the written word

Many teachers believe that young learners should learn to listen and speak in English before they experience the written word. Others maintain that encountering written English early on is not harmful, and is even desirable.

For those teachers who are open to the use of written texts in activities, here are a few techniques for introducing writing:

- encourage awareness of print—let the children see you use the written word
- encourage pre-writing activities in which the children may say they are writing, although you may not recognize it as such
- encourage the children to recognize individual letters, particularly to be able to write their name
- encourage the copying of sentences or phrases

- encourage playing with letter shapes, so the children become familiar with the essential character of letters
- write or type out the children's stories, and read them back to them.

Writing can be dropped from, or included in, almost every activity in this book. It's up to you!

Discrete activities and integrated activities

The character of a resource book for teachers is that the activities can be taken in any order, and fitted by the teacher into his or her lesson plans. I am very aware that many teachers like the children to perceive activities as being linked, and part of a more comprehensive experience. It certainly makes sense for the children, since having experiences which overlap, and relate to or reinforce each other will help to build up their understanding. They will also respond more creatively if they feel 'at home' with the topic. For these reasons, I am including here a suggestion of how art, design, and language development might be linked with a wide variety of subjects and activities.

A linking theme can be a story which the children invent themselves. They can focus on subjects the story touches on as they progress, for example, how the animals in the story live. Then you can give them the opportunity to produce drawings, maps, and posters, and even create a small exhibition.

Cross-curricular responsibilities

I believe passionately in the idea that language development, be it in the mother tongue or a foreign language, should be experienced as part of the child's overall development. Of course, cross-curricular work is the characteristic way in which much teaching of *young* children has been done over many years.

However, as with all powerful notions, this approach has a good side and a bad side. The bad side, in this case, is that as a language teaching specialist I may not be sufficiently informed about, and sensitive to, the concerns of specialists in other aspects of the curriculum I wish to involve. The following paragraphs are addressed in particular to those teachers who want to involve art and design in their language teaching, but feel less than well-informed about the principles of art, crafts, and design education.

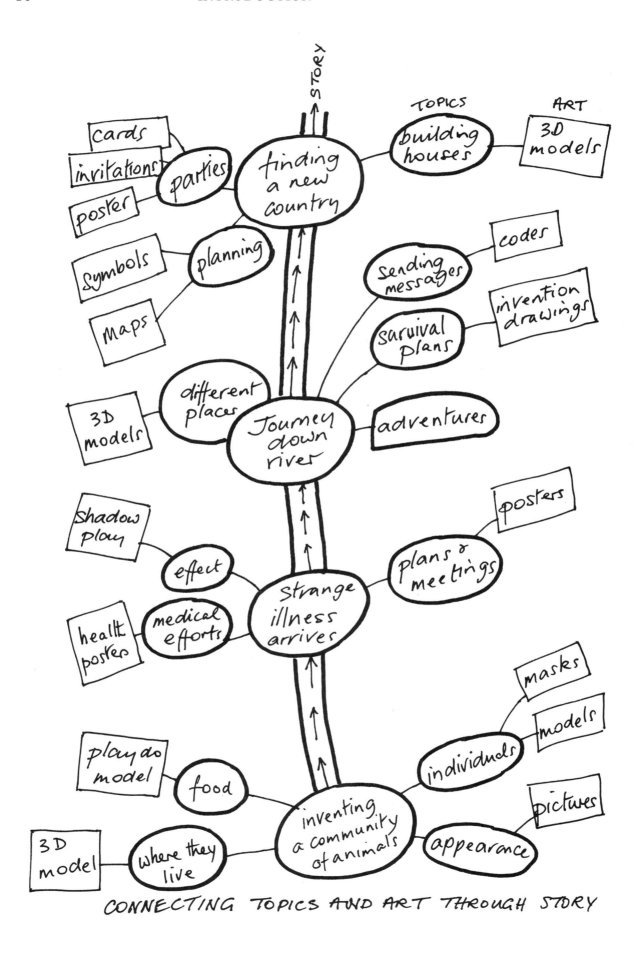

CONNECTING TOPICS AND ART THROUGH STORY

Specialist teachers

The ideal situation is one in which an art specialist is willing to combine their lesson time and resources and, above all, their vision and experience, with yours.

The advantages of cooperation are as follows:
– your lesson time is effectively 'doubled'
– you can draw on the expertise and interest of the other teacher
– you have access to far more resources, in terms of materials and equipment
– you can provide meaningful activities for the children in which they experience the foreign language as being important in different ways
– the work can be your contribution to the current drive in primary education worldwide to develop cross-curricular work.

Even if you cannot join forces with an art specialist, you can still use the activities in this book, particularly if you follow the suggestions in the instructions for the individual activities.

Is there right and wrong, good and bad in art?

Art and design are physical manifestations of thinking and feeling. If this premise is accepted, we must understand that when we evaluate art and design, we are evaluating thinking and feeling. So the question becomes 'What are good thoughts and feelings?'

Doesn't the answer largely depend on the context? For example, a cheerful remark may be perfect at one moment, but quite inappropriate at another. Rembrandt's studies, explanatory diagrams, and cartoons can all be 'right' in different contexts.

 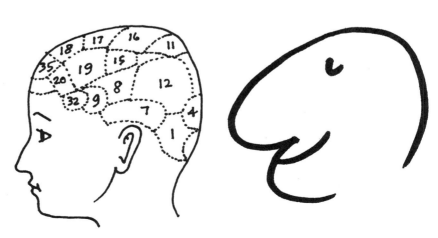

However, there *are* forms of thinking and of drawing which I feel are always undesirable: boastful, deceitful, slick ideas do not help many people. Art, like any other human activity, is full of such things—surely we should not give such attitudes and ideas any encouragement!

Clichés may be regarded as sensitive, and even profound, by the uninformed. However, they actually contribute little, because they are not derived directly from experience. They are passed on as phrases or as images—basically, we all know them and they tell us nothing new. To teach children tricks for drawing horses' heads, for example, prevents them from developing a sense of drawing as a whole. This is rather like only teaching a few fixed phrases in English, and not helping the children to experience how the language works. While a few tricks can be quite useful at times, the main thrust of our work throughout the curriculum must be in helping the children to develop as thinking and feeling people, not merely manipulators of essentially low-level techniques.

There are some suggestions in the activities in this book for helping children to judge the character or shapes of objects. I do not say that 'you must draw a bird by drawing two ovals, one for its head and one for its body'—that would be a trick. What I say is that every animal and object has its shape, and that it is helpful when reproducing a shape to relate it to rectangles, triangles, or circles. There is plenty of opportunity when using this technique for studying, reflecting, and making decisions—a technique is not necessarily a trick. Cézanne found cubes in nature, but he also emphasized the importance of 'going back to nature', i.e. of looking at nature, and indeed all personal experience, and trying to make sense of it. It is this balance which I believe in. Use a map, by all means, but eventually you will have to get off the beaten track and see what you can discover for yourself.

It can be very easy to assume that art and design should *always* be pushing forward the frontiers of experience. There *are* times when we need an easily recognizable picture—for example, on road signs! In some contexts, a well-known and readily recognizable image can turn out to be 'the best picture'.

So, in conclusion, we are left with the same criteria for evaluating art that we would use when evaluating any other human thinking and communication activity. Broadly speaking, people who are familiar with art, and who give it high value in their lives, are likely to judge a picture as 'good' if the shapes, colours, lines, and textures are arranged in a characterful relationship with each other. The same is true if the medium of expression is used with sensitivity and delight—but then, that applies to all communication!

Copying and colouring-in

Copying is a natural part of development, particularly if it is selective copying rather than an attempt to make a replica. However, constant copying without reflection produces dependence on others, and the regurgitation of existing forms and ideas.

Colouring-in printed line pictures is very common: most children enjoy it. Most children also enjoy eating chocolate and sucking lollipops, but we all know that such things are damaging to their health! Colouring-in, like copying, leads to an extremely narrow concept of art, unless they want to colour-in their own drawings, which is, of course, quite a different matter.

My policy with my own children is to accept a certain amount of chocolate eating, and colouring-in of pictures, but to do my best—not always successfully—to offer enticing alternatives that are more likely to be beneficial for their minds and bodies.

Responding to the children's work

Talking about pictures in a foreign language is not easy. The most important thing is not to encourage the children to think that the main aims in art are photographic realism, slickness, and neatness. Frequently, asking the question: *What's this?* makes children think that making something naturalistically recognizable is the only purpose in art.

If you want to compliment a child, say:

What a lovely picture!
What an interesting idea!
That's a frightening robot!

If you want the child to talk about his or her picture, say:

Tell me about your picture rather than *What is it?*

If you want to respond to the quality of the painting, say:

I love these colours here! They are so rich!
Are the colours and shapes happy/unhappy angry?

If the picture has a design purpose:

Tell me about your picture.
What is this picture for?
What do you want them to think/feel/do?
Can people see it?
Can people understand it?

If you want to respond to what he/she might do with the picture:

I think your mum and dad will love this picture.

Who do you want to see this picture?
Where do you want to put it?
You can put it on the wall in your kitchen/bedroom.
Can I put your picture on the wall in the classroom?

If you want the child to get away from clichés and stereotypes, say:

Look at the houses/trees/clouds/flowers through the window. They are all special.
Tell me about this part of the picture (rather than *What's this?*).
Is that Mary or Jenny? Do Mary and Jenny look the same? What's the difference?

If you want to respond negatively, I would suggest that you do so through questions which help the child to realize for him or herself what is unsatisfactory:

Teacher: *What do you want to show in your picture?*
Child: *John.*
Teacher: *Has John got a fat face or a thin face?*
Child: *A thin face.*
Teacher: *Is this face a fat or a thin face?*
Child: *A fat face.*
Teacher: *Do you want to make it thinner?*

She's an artist!

One of the worst things we can do to children is to label them, and it's just as bad to label them a 'good artist' as a 'bad artist'. When a *good artist* becomes the *class artist*, the child is trapped in that role, while calling a child a *poor artist* is enough to make anyone give up altogether!

The best way of acknowledging a child's gifts is to respond with joy to what they produce:

What a lovely picture! Let's put it on the wall so that other people can see it and enjoy it (*enjoy* rather than *admire*).

The polished product

It is very tempting to only praise and display work which looks clever and neat, because this can impress some people, and reflect well on the teacher. After all, teachers need praise and acknowledgement, too! However, we must remember that the most important responsibility we have is to ensure that our children develop as rich and responsible individuals: 20 butterflies, neatly drawn by you, and neatly coloured in by the children, represent 20 minds being led one step nearer to accepting the ordinary and the shallow!

Teach them or let them discover for themselves?

Both are important. Teaching (i.e. telling, explaining, and demonstrating) can be offered at the point where the child has a conscious need for help. For example, if you want the children to draw butterflies, look at a photograph of a butterfly together (or, if you are lucky, the real thing). Talk about the shape and size of its wings compared with its slim little body, and then ask the children to draw it. This is when language has a most important role in guiding and inspiring.

Art for communication

Drawing is usually thought of as a form of personal expression which other people might or might not understand and enjoy. However, drawing and designing can also be used as a way of communicating a specific idea which is readily understood by other people. Developing communication skills in children must be one of the most important of our tasks in school.

Communication skills require an awareness and understanding of content, audience, and medium/design. Here is an example:

Designing and drawing picture symbols
Content: What are the most obvious visual features of the person or thing to be communicated? From which viewpoint?
Audience: What will they recognize easily? What will they understand and care about?
Medium/design: Colour or black and white? Size? Needs to be visible from a distance, perhaps from a moving vehicle, or from nearby?

Publishing, performing, and displaying

Traditionally, the only receiver of a child's communication in school was the teacher. I believe it is most important for children to learn how to communicate with a wider variety of people, and in a broader context than the classroom. Art and crafts lend themselves to this wider form of communication. They can be displayed in many places, for example, in the school lobby, the local bank or store, or a community hall. Publishing (making the children's texts and pictures available in book form) can lead to books being put in the school library, and the local bookshop or coffee bar.

Art and crafts can contribute to dramatic performances, too. Make-up, the creation of masks, costumes, and props, and the designing and painting of backdrops, all require creative input.

Through all these activities, the children can have the pleasure of seeing that their work is appreciated. At the same time, they can experience the responsibility of trying to do a good job in their communication with other people.

Parents and colleagues

It is important that the parents and your colleagues respect, or, at least accept, what you are doing! Parents often criticize the 'songs and games' approach to primary language teaching, claiming that although the children may be having lots of fun, they are not making much progress. You need to make it clear to them that your approach involves integrated, cross-curricular activities. Take every opportunity to demonstrate that the children are developing their language proficiency through these activities (see 'Publishing, performing, and displaying', above). You might also produce a 'rationale' for doing what you are doing. Here is a draft version which you might like to adapt:

Language is meaningful to children when it is experienced as an important part of an activity which matters to them individually.

Children feel that creative art activities are interesting and enjoyable. They therefore offer a powerful way of integrating language and action.

The added advantage of creative art activities is that the relatively limited language proficiency of the children is not a drawback!

How to use this book

How this book is organized

Chapter headings: media

I felt that the best way of grouping the activities was according to the medium concerned, for example, *Three-dimensional activities*, *Printing*, and *Colours*. Since any one activity might contain several themes and language teaching points, these did not seem to provide a useful way of organizing the book.

Appendix: Materials and techniques

Suggestions for useful materials to bring to the class, their basic characteristics, and what you might do with them.

How each activity is organized

Level

The level given is only an approximation. Slight changes to the activity can make it more or less demanding. If the children in your class have not started writing, leave out that aspect of the activity. If they have not started using a past–tense form, use a present–tense form. If you play a bigger role in the activity, giving more language, writing useful words and phrases on the board, or doing brief practice activities, you can help lower-proficiency children to do the same activity as a more advanced group.

The levels in this book are as follows:

Beginners

This category ranges from children with little or no knowledge of English to those who have been learning it for about a year. Their active use of the language will be very limited, and they may not be able to make full sentences.

Elementary

These children are able to use English more actively, and to make simple sentences and questions. They will have a wider range of vocabulary.

Pre-intermediate

These children will be more capable of recognizing sentence patterns, and more willing to 'have a go' at generating language of their own. They are ready to learn structures such as the past simple and comparatives, as well as functional language for expressing obligation, making requests and suggestions, and so on.

Age
The age given is only approximate. Younger children can do their version of the activity, and older children can use a more sophisticated version.

Aims
Language: These cover language and skills development. Only the key language focus is given. The point of doing 'real' activities is that they invite the use of a whole range of functions and language.
Other: These involve the intellectual and social development of the children.

Time
A rough guide only. Please note that many of the activities can be done as ongoing projects over several lessons.

Materials
In general, the materials required are easy to find.

Preparation
In most cases there is something for you to do beforehand, but the preparation is straightforward.

In class
A step-by-step guide to what you do in class. No doubt you will adjust these suggestions to your own style, and to the needs of the class.

Variations
Alternative ways of doing the activity.

Follow-up(s)
Some other activities you might do, once you have completed the main activity.

1 Three-dimensional activities

Children, particularly young ones, love to get hold of things. The solidity of three-dimensional objects gives a reality to the language they use in association with those objects. Feeling an object as well as seeing it, and using it for a particular purpose, helps to reinforce the language associated with it in the learner's memory.

1.1 Binoculars and telescopes

Looking through binoculars (or a telescope) and reporting what you see is a perfect situation for the use of the present continuous to refer to actions taking place at the moment.

LEVEL

Beginners and elementary

AGE

4–12

AIMS

Language: to practise the present continuous form of a variety of verbs of action.
Other: to experience the effect of focusing on objects at a distance.

TIME

30–40 minutes

MATERIALS

Cardboard tubes, 10 to 15 cm long (two for each pair of children), coloured paper, glue or sticky tape, scissors, cling film, and a brush for sweeping up afterwards. If you don't have enough cardboard tubes, let the children make telescopes instead.

PREPARATION

Make a model pair of binoculars to show the children. If you have a real pair of binoculars, bring them in as well.

IN CLASS

1 Show the children your finished pair of binoculars. Look through them at the children, and identify who you can see and what they are doing.

   Teacher: *I can see Tibor. He's laughing and he's waving!*

2 Let one of the children look through the binoculars.

   Teacher: *Who can you see?*
   Child: *Alex.*

Teacher: *What is she doing?*
Child: *She's smiling.*

3 Write sample sentences on the board, for example:

He's laughing.
She's waving.
She's smiling.

4 Brainstorm all the actions the children can do, and the English words for the actions.

5 Continue to let more children have a go, using the model sentences on the board to guide their answers. Some children can take over your role of asking questions.

6 Help the children to make binoculars for themselves.

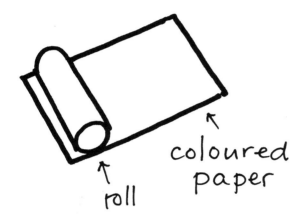

Useful language:

Take the coloured paper/cling film.
Put the roll on the paper.
Cut the paper.
Stick the paper on the roll.
Stick the cling film on the ends of each roll.
Stick the two rolls together with sticky tape.

7 The children use their binoculars in pairs, basing their questions and answers on the model on the board.

VARIATION 1

Move into the use of the past simple tense when someone does a sequence of actions. The children identify, remember, and report on what happened.

Fold a piece of A5 paper. Draw a circle on the fold. Cut out the circle. Open out the paper, and you will have two round holes.

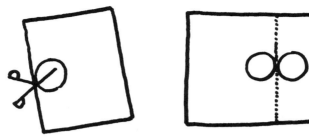

Ask: *(Name of child), What can you see?*

The child gives an imaginative reply, for example: *I can see five pirates.*

FOLLOW-UP 1

Follow-up this activity with the listening game, in which all the children close their eyes and listen to noises being made by you or by one or two children, accompanied by the question, *What am I doing?*

The children answer as appropriate, for example: *You are walking. You are coughing. You are laughing. You are jumping. You are talking.*

1.2 Cars

The children make cars and then 'drive' them, using English while they are making the cars, giving directions, and talking about road safety.

LEVEL

Elementary and above

AGE

4–12

AIMS

Language: to revise and practise vocabulary for parts of a car, for driving, and for giving instructions.
Other: to make a large model; to use knives and scissors safely; to practise road safety rules.

TIME

60 minutes for making the cars; 20 minutes for playing with them (or more if you have time)

MATERIALS

For each group of four children:
One large cardboard box (car body), 5 paper plates (wheels and steering wheel), 2 aluminium foil cooking dishes or white plastic yoghurt tops (lights), about 1m of thick string, a strip of white card or a narrow card tray (number plate), wire paper clips, glue, a craft knife, and scissors.

If you want the children to paint the cars, you will also need powder paints and water, brushes, aprons, and a plastic covering.

PREPARATION

Cut a hole in the bottom of each box, big enough for a child's body to fit through it. Cut off the upper flaps.

For young children, you will need to do all the rest of the cutting beforehand, but for older groups, use your judgement as to how much they can safely do on their own.

IN CLASS

1 With the hole at the top, the children paint the car.

2 With the scissors, make a small hole for each of the wheel axles in the sides of the box. Now make holes in the four plates. Fasten the wire paper clips through the paper plates, and attach them to the car.

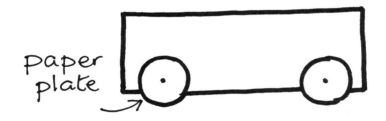

3 Fasten the two aluminium foil cooking dishes to the front of the car to represent lights.

4 Glue the white rectangle of card on the back of the car for the registration plate. Write on it the initial letters of each child's name, and a number.

5 Glue the fifth paper plate on the top of the front of the car to represent a steering wheel.

6 Make two holes with the scissors through the upper part of the car, in the centre. Pass the thick string through each hole and

tie the ends together. There should be enough string to pass up the front of the child's chest, behind his or her neck, back down the front of the chest, and through the hole in the top of the car.

7 When the cars are ready, make roads in the classroom between the tables, or with chalk outside on the playground. Let the children take turns to be drivers and pedestrians, practising road safety, and giving directions.

1.3 Clay animal

It is important to give children the opportunity to model objects in three dimensions, as well as to experience the feel of clay (or alternative materials—see Appendix, page 136). In this activity, each of the children makes an imaginary animal.

LEVEL

Beginners

AGE

5–12

AIMS

Language: to practise vocabulary for parts of the body and for proportions and shapes.
Other: to make models with clay; to observe and judge size, shape, and proportion.

TIME

30 minutes to make the animal

MATERIALS

Enough clay or other modelling material for each child to have a piece the size of their fist, aprons, protective plastic, or old newspapers, wet cloths, and a bucket of water, etc.

IN CLASS

1 Put a wooden board or a piece of newspaper on each child's desk (to keep it clean). Give each child a piece of clay.
2 Ask the children to close their eyes, feel the clay, and play with it.
3 The children open their eyes. Tell them that you are going to help them to invent their own animal. They will have to get their clay ready, enough for each part of the animal. They also

have to decide how big each part of the body must be, and how much clay they need for it. Say things like:

Has your animal got a big head or a little head?
A big head, Evelyn? OK, you take a big piece of clay.
A small head, John? OK, you take a small piece of clay.
Has your animal got a big body or a small body?
Take a big/small piece of clay.
How many legs has it got? John, six? Take six pieces of clay.

4 Organize the order in which the children make their animals. Avoid interfering with their interpretation of the shape of the animal they want to make.

Now let's make the body of the animal. Has it got a big fat body, or a little fat body or a long fat body, or a long thin body? Is it round or is it flat?

Circulate, talking to the children. Ask them to talk about the shape of their animal's body by giving them a lot of alternatives. This makes them reply with a full sentence, rather than with 'yes' or 'no'.

5 When most of the children are ready, ask them to go on to make the head, and after that the legs. Technically, the main help the children need will be in making good joints between the different parts by smoothing down the clay where the two parts join. Continue to use the vocabulary of shape and size.

6 The children can now add extra features, for example, wings, ears, horns, and teeth. They can also press the ends of pencils, and the edges of coins, etc. into their animals to create textures.

7 Finally, the children can paint their animals, even when the clay is still wet.

8 Find somewhere safe for the animals to dry.

FOLLOW-UP 1

The children can display their animals and then take it in turns to describe one of them for another child to identify.

Child A: *It has a small head and a long, round body, and eight short legs.*
Child B: *This one?*
Child A: *No, not that one.*
Child B: *This one?*
Child A: *Yes!*

FOLLOW-UP 2

The children can study how real animals are described, and then invent a description of their animal. Here is a description of a real animal which you can give the children as a model:

> **LIONS**
> Lions live in Africa.
> Lions are very strong and they can run very fast.
> Lions are yellow and brown.
> Lions hunt and eat animals, for example, zebras and deer.
> The daddy (male) lion sleeps all day.
> The mummy (female) lion hunts and gives the food to the daddy.
> The daddy lion has a lot of hair on his head.
> The mummy lion doesn't have a lot of hair on her head.
> Baby lions are called cubs. They look sweet and they play a lot.

COMMENTS

See page 139 in the Appendix for advice on the use of clay and other materials.

1.4 Clay food

The children study the shapes of different foods, then make them out of clay or similar material, and paint them.

LEVEL

All

AGE

5–12

AIMS

Language: to practise vocabulary for food, and for the shapes of different types of food, for example *bananas, apples, loaves of bread, cakes, biscuits, sandwiches; round, long, short, thin, flat.*
Other: to observe the differences between the shapes and colours of various types of fruit.

TIME

90 minutes

MATERIALS

A variety of foods, for example: bread, cake, sandwich, pizza, hot dog, orange, lemon, banana, pineapple, apple, pear, etc.

Clay, plasticine, modelling clay, or play-dough—enough to give each child an amount about as big as an egg. (For more about these materials and how to make play-dough, see the Appendix, page 139.)

Aprons, protective plastic, or old newspapers, wet cloths, and a bucket of water.

PREPARATION

You can ask the children to bring in some of the types of food.

IN CLASS

1 Arrange four tables in the middle of the room. The children's tables can remain scattered around rather than in a circle.

2 With the children's help, arrange the various foods on the central tables. In this way, revise or teach the words for them.

Informally, you might also express likes and dislikes for the food.

3 Teach or revise the words for the shapes of the various types of food by describing them, and by asking the children to say what you are describing.

Teacher: *It's long and it's curved.*
Child: *It's the banana.*

Then let them take over your role.

4 Put a board or piece of newspaper on each desk for each pair of children. Add a piece of clay about the size of an egg for each child.

5 Now tell the children that they are going to make food out of the clay. Help each child to decide what to make: try to make sure that a wide variety of foods is included. The children can say what they are going to do by playing the 'describe and identify' game: *they* describe and *you* try to identify the food.

6 The children go to the central tables to study the food they have chosen (without picking it up). They then make the food. Circulate and talk to each pair of children, helping them to look critically at what they are making in relation to the actual object.

Is it a carrot? What is it? What shape is a banana? Is your banana curved and long?

7 Having got the basic shape of the food right, the children can add texture to the food, such as tiny holes in the skin of an orange. Then they can paint the food quite thickly with a water-based paint.

8 When everybody is ready, invite half the children to walk around and look at everybody else's food, and to identify the different foods.

Child A: *What's that?*
Child B: *It's an orange.*

(*Note*: the focus of this activity is to represent the appearance of particular objects, and not to express feelings about them. So if it is not absolutely clear, it is quite natural for the children to ask *What's that?*)

9 Collect the foods and find a place to let them dry safely. Exhibit the foods with labels, for example:

Julie's orange. It is round and orange.
This is a pizza. It is round and flat. It is John's pizza.

FOLLOW-UP

The models of food items can be used for various other purposes, for example:
- grouping in various ways and explaining the grouping
- shopping and shopping lists
- parties
- restaurant role play.

1.5 Mobile phone

A mobile phone offers a natural situation for describing something which the listener cannot see, using the present continuous tense

LEVEL   **All**

AGE   4–12

AIMS   **Language:** to practise using the present continuous tense.
Other: to practise using a telephone.

TIME   **30 minutes to make the mobile phone**

MATERIALS   For each pair of children:
a small juice carton (250 ml), coloured paper, sticky tape, a straw, squares of gummed paper.

PREPARATION   Make up one mobile phone before the class:
1 Wrap the box in coloured paper and secure it with sticky tape.
2 Attach a straw for the aerial.
3 Cut out shapes from the gummed paper and stick them on to represent the buttons.

IN CLASS
1 Show the class the mobile phone you have made and pretend to have a conversation with someone, perhaps a parent. For example:

Hello! Is it Mrs Jennings? Is Kate here? Yes, I think she's here. Yes, there she is! What's she doing? Oh, she's smiling! Nice girl? Sometimes! Sometimes, she's a nice girl!
John? Yes, he's here somewhere ... oh, there he is! He's sitting at the back of the class. Yes. What's he doing? He's smiling as well ... oh ... now he's laughing! Oh, now he's jumping and waving. OK! Bye, bye!

2 Put some of the useful phrases on the board:

Is she here? Yes, she's here.
What's she doing? She's smiling.
She is a nice girl. She isn't a nice girl.

Let one or two children practise doing the same sort of phone conversation.

This will establish the idea of playing with the mobile and wanting one.

3 Help the children to make a mobile phone. It is best to do it step by step, making sure that every child is keeping up with you, and does a reasonable job. Make sure you keep to the same instructional phrases if possible, and use a lot of language of praise and encouragement.

Put the piece of coloured paper on the table.
Put the box on the paper.
Fold the paper round the box.
That's good. That's right.

4 Encourage the children to play with the phones, making use of the sentences you have put on the board.

5 The children will soon want to deviate from this conversation. Ask them to work in pairs to invent a new conversation, rehearse it, and then act it out for the class. While they are practising, the children can sit back-to-back. When performing in front of the class, they can sit further apart.

1.6   Roll sentences

The children write and illustrate sentences in strips which can be rotated around a cardboard tube to make new sentences. These rolls allow the children to manipulate sentence patterns, which is especially helpful for the many children who learn best by being able to touch and move something. Parts of the sentence should be illustrated rather than written.

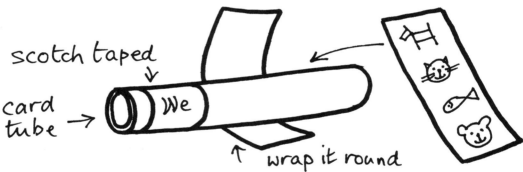

LEVEL	**Elementary and above**
AGE	7–12
AIMS	**Language:** reading and writing; practising sentence patterns the children are familiar with.
TIME	**45 minutes**
MATERIALS	A cardboard roll of any diameter, about 20 cm long, for each child or pair of children. The alternative to cardboard rolls are lengths of plastic or metal piping.

A large cardboard roll to use as a class example. The largest ones are used for carpets – which can be many metres long!

A large number of strips of paper, and sticky tape to fasten them around the roll.

PREPARATION

If you are able to obtain a large roll, prepare some strips of paper by writing on them the words of sentences such as *I like chocolate*, *I have got a dog*, and stick them around the roll, as shown in the illustration.

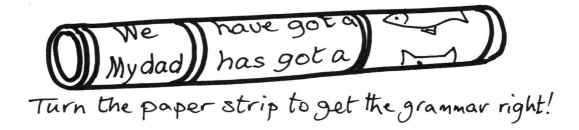

Turn the paper strip to get the grammar right!

IN CLASS

1 If you have made a roll, show it to the class. Ask two children to hold either end of it. Ask another child to turn the circular strips of paper, and to read out some of the sentences which are formed as the words and pictures create new combinations.

2 Ask the class to tell you some of the sentences they have just heard, and write them on the board. Invite the children to suggest alternative words for each part of the sentences they have remembered.

3 Each of the pairs, or groups of three, makes a sentence roll, guided by the sentences and alternative words written on the board. Because each part of the sentence is on a strip of its own, each child can contribute at the same time by writing the appropriate words, or drawing the appropriate pictures.

4 Pairs or groups visit each other and play with their sentence rolls, discussing which is the funniest sentence.

VARIATION 3

Any pictures, words, and phrases can be written on the strips of paper. The strips can be rotated to offer ideas for storytelling.

Invent a story based on the pictures.

Alternatively, a complete text can be written out, cut into strips, and rotated around the roll until all the words are in the right sequence.

1.7 See through the paper

Here are two ways of using both sides of the paper at the same time! In the first case, the children draw on one side of the paper, hold it against a window, and write on the other side. In the variation, they pierce a picture with a pin, and on the other side of the paper write down the word for the object which has been pierced.

LEVEL

Beginners and elementary

AGE

4–12

AIMS

Language: to practise using descriptive words and phrases, spoken or written; to learn/revise the names of facial features.
Other: to develop appreciation of the variety of the character of materials, and of their potential.

TIME

30 minutes

MATERIALS

An A4 sheet of plain white paper for each child.

For the variation: a pin, and a reproduction of a painting, for example on a postcard, for each child.

PREPARATION

Try the activity and the variation before the lesson. They are much easier to do than to describe!

IN CLASS

1 Draw a face on a piece of A4 paper. As you do so, describe each part: *Here is the face. Here are the eyes—one eye, two eyes, …*

2 When you have done the drawing, test the children's memory of the vocabulary for the facial features.

3 Gather the children around in a semicircle, so that they are facing a window.

4 Place the paper against the window, with the picture of the face against the glass. You and the children will see the drawing quite clearly through the paper. Ask again what each feature is in English. Write the answers down, on the *back* of the paper, and on top of the features.

5 Ask two children to sit at the front of the semicircle, one with his/her back to the window, and one facing him/her. Ask the

child facing the window to hold the paper with the words written on his/her side.

6 The child with his/her back to the window can now see the drawing, but not the words! He or she should point to the different facial features and, touching the paper, say the name of each feature. The child on the other side will see the finger's shadow touching the facial feature, and will be able to check the word given with the word written.

She can see the picture through the paper and the words on the back.

light

window

He can only see the picture on the paper. He points at parts of the picture and tries to name them.

VARIATION

1 Give each child or pair of children a reproduction of a painting in which there are at least five things which the children can usefully name.

2 The children should pierce through the objects, one by one, with a pin.

3 Next to the pinhole, on the other side of the paper, the children should write the word for the object, for example, *window*.

4 The children can then sit in pairs, facing each other. Child **A** with his/her back to the light can see the picture, but not the words. Child **B** can see the pinpricks of light and the words written on the back.

5 **A** points at an object, covering the pin-prick hole with his or her finger, and says the word or phrase for it. **B** sees the pinprick of light disappear, hears the word, and checks it with what is written.

1.8 This isn't a pen

The children play with the idea that objects are not what they seem, but something else! Art and design essentially involves seeing a medium both as itself, and as something else, at the same time.

This idea is natural for children (who will happily sit in a cardboard box and say it is a house) but more difficult for adults to grasp.

LEVEL   **Beginners and upwards**

AGE

4–12 for the introductory activity.
8–12 upwards for the variation, as young children do not find it easy to fasten one object to another.

AIMS

Language: to practise negative and positive statements in the present tense, and the indefinite article:

This isn't a pen. It's a knife!
This isn't a piece of paper. It's an umbrella!

Other: to encourage the children to be imaginative.

TIME

20 minutes

MATERIALS

A pen, an A4 sheet of paper, something to fasten things together, for example glue, string, staples.

A rubbish collection, as described in the Appendix, page 137.

IN CLASS

1 Show the children the pen and ask them what it is.

 Teacher: *What's this?*
 Child: *It's a pen!*
 Teacher: *No, it isn't!* (pretending to use it like a knife) *It's a knife!*

 Then balance the piece of paper on your finger, like an umbrella. Tell them: *This isn't a piece of paper! It's an umbrella!*

2 Tell the children to work in pairs. They should each take an object they have with them, imagine it is something else, and demonstrate it to their partner.

3 Some children should demonstrate theirs to the class as a whole.

4 The children can then make animals and objects out of items from your rubbish collection. Remind them that Picasso's famous bull was made out of a bicycle saddle and handlebars!

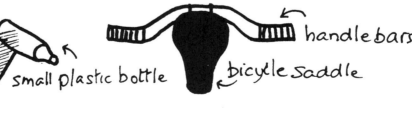

If they have started writing, the children can write captions under their rubbish sculpture:

This is a bull.
The head is a bicycle saddle.
The horns are bicycle handlebars.

This is a giraffe.
The neck is a cardboard roll.
The body is a turnip.

The legs are pencils.
The head is a bottle.

VARIATION

Use the plural form. For example:

Teacher: *What are these?* (showing your fingers)
Child: *Fingers.*
Teacher: *No, they aren't fingers!* (making each thumb and forefinger into circles and putting them over your eyes) *They're glasses!*

COMMENTS

As and when the children need it, this is a very good way of teaching new vocabulary.

1.9   Town and country setting

For many children, experience comes alive when they can hold and move something. If you have your own classroom, consider making a landscape or a townscape, and letting the children play with it. Language will be used in the making of the place, when describing it, and when living out imaginary events that might be taking place in it.

LEVEL

Elementary and above

AGE

4–12

AIMS

Language: *What's this? It's a ....*
You can drive on this road. You can stop here. You can go into this house.
Vocabulary of natural and man-made features in a landscape. Daily routines. Prepositions. Past-tense adventures. Dramatic dialogues.
Other: to make models; to help children develop awareness of their surroundings.

TIME

90 minutes + to prepare the setting. After that, many activities can be based on it

MATERIALS

These are the materials for a simple setting, but your and the children's imaginations should not be limited by this list!

One large table, or two desks together, to provide a support.
A piece of white card or thick paper to provide the basis for the setting.
Thin card to be cut, folded, stuck, and painted for houses, bridges, trees, bridges, boats, etc.
A collection of cardboard boxes to be used for cars, buses, buildings, etc.
Paints, glue, scissors, craft knives.
Aprons, protective plastic, a broom, etc.

Copies of Worksheets 1.9A and B (pages 145–6)

PREPARATION

Make sure there are a couple of spare desks or a large table in the room, where the model can be kept safely for some weeks.

IN CLASS

1 Discuss with the children what they might like to make: a mixture of town, country, and sea or lake gives lots of flexibility. Talk about what should be in the setting: natural features (hills, rivers, etc.), man-made features (roads, bridges, railways, old and modern buildings, for example, a castle, a supermarket, a farm). Help to organize who should do what. Make sure that all the children keep to a similar scale, so that the supermarket, for example, shouldn't be smaller than a tree.

2 Get the children started. Depending on their age, you might like to give out Worksheets 1.9A and B.

3 While the children are painting the setting, showing the roads and rivers, and making the objects, use language in the following ways:

Identifying:
What this? It's a ...
Look everybody! John is making a ...

Encouraging:
It's very nice/beautiful/well-made!

Helping:
Is it the right size? Too big/too small?
Cut it like this.

VARIATIONS

The most practical way of making a setting has been described above. However, there are other very practical methods, and they are summarized here:

Sand
Nursery and infant schools often have a sand tray in the classroom, or a sandpit outside the classroom. With damp sand, the children can make roads, tunnels, hills, and ponds. Toys can be used for buildings, cars, and people, or they can be made from card.

Papier mâché
This material can be used to make a very durable and flexible setting (see the Appendix, page 137, for how to make it). Hills, rivers, houses, trees, etc. can be made and painted most realistically. But, of course, it takes longer to do.

Saltdough
This can be used for objects, such as houses (see the Appendix, page 140, for how to make it).

Miniature environments
A cooking tin or baking tray can be used to hold a miniature garden: earth, a clod of grass, flowers, stones, even a miniature pond. The children study life in their garden, recording it in an objective way, or making up stories about imaginary people who live there.

FOLLOW-UP

Use the setting for:
- identifying
- imaginary dialogues, for example, giving directions
- building up a soap-opera community: daily routines, jobs, hobbies, shopping, stories.

2 Puppets, masks, and manikins

Many children 'come to life' when the focus is taken off them, and they can speak unselfconsciously through a puppet, a mask, or a manikin (a model of a human being). The puppet, mask, and manikin can remain with the child throughout his or her study of English. As the child learns more and more language, so he or she can say more and more about the puppet. In the first week of English, the puppet can simply acquire a name. As the months go by, the child can talk and write about what it does every day, what pets it has, what its favourite food is, and so on.

In this section, a few pointers are given for how this relationship might be achieved. In *Drama with Children* by Sarah Phillips (in this series—see other titles in the Resource Books for Teachers series on page 142), there is an extensive section on making and using puppets, while in their book *Very Young Learners* (also in this series), Vanessa Riley and Sheila Ward have some useful suggestions for making and using animal masks. I have tried not to overlap with the many excellent suggestions given in these books.

2.1 Puppets

This activity focuses on the making of puppets, and ideas for using them. Home-made puppets have two advantages over ready-made ones: first, there is the fun of making them, and then the challenge of creating characters for them.

I suggest that the children should make animals rather than 'people' puppets. If the children like the idea of inventing an animal, they could also invent the name of the species: a cross between a dog and a cat, for example, can become a 'dat' or a 'cog'! Inventing an animal offers the advantage of not having to be particularly realistic. On the other hand, many young children prefer the comfort of a known animal as their 'English pet'. Be open to both possibilities.

LEVEL	**All**
AGE	4–12
AIMS	**Language:** to practise oral fluency, followed by written fluency and accuracy. If the puppet is kept and used as a basis of more

work in the future, a whole range of language items and functions
can be practised with it.

Other: to make and work with puppets.

TIME	**60–80 minutes**
MATERIALS	Scraps of paper, cloth, cardboard (including rolls), wool, cork, etc. glue, string, sticky tape, and a stapler, one A3 sheet of paper for each child, copies of Worksheet 2.1 (page 147) for ideas on making puppets out of scrap material.
PREPARATION	Make a puppet of your own to take to the lesson.

IN CLASS

1 Show the children your puppet. Get them to ask the puppet
questions with the English they have. The puppet can ask the
children questions, too (you ask the questions through the
puppet). You may like to write questions on the board. Also, get
the puppet to speak to individual children.

Here are some simple questions:

Hello, what's your name?
How old are you?
Have you got a brother or a sister?
What's your hobby?
What's your favourite food/music/sport, etc.
Do you like swimming?

For invented animals:

What is your father? What is your mother?
What are you?

More demanding questions to ask and to answer:

What did you do this morning?
Where do you go for your holidays?
Which television programmes do you watch?
What makes you frightened/angry/sad?
What do you want to do/have/be?
What difficulties do you have?

2 Tell the children that you want each of them to make a puppet
from the materials provided. They should finish the puppet by
drawing or painting the eyes and other details. If their pens
don't draw on the material they have used, they may have to
stick paper onto the puppet, and draw and paint on that.

The children must try to make their puppets in 30 minutes.
(You can, of course, allow much more time if you wish, and let
the making of puppets become a significant topic activity. Very
young children are not likely to respond to the idea of a time
limit.)

While the children are making the puppets there is an
opportunity to use language to help and encourage them:

That's nice. Well done. Cut it carefully. Glue it well. Tie it well. This can be the head. These can be the legs. Is this his head? Are these his legs?

3 As the children finish their puppets, they can show them to each other. Encourage them to imagine the character of their puppets, and to speak to each other through them.

4 When all the puppets are ready, ask the children to sit in a circle. Invite one child to say, through his or her puppet, who he or she would like to meet from amongst the other puppets, for example:

Child: *I would like to meet Mary's puppet.*

5 These two children and their puppets should then sit opposite each other in the centre of the circle. One half of the class (making up one half of the circle) sits behind one child, and the other half of the class sits behind the other child. It is a good idea to ask each of the two children to show their puppet to their half of the class before going any further.

6 The two children then begin their conversation, using whatever English they have, and asking you for any words they need.

The children sitting behind each child can also ask the other puppet questions. This is an opportunity for you to help the children to realize the range of subjects which they can attempt with their limited amount of English. It is also a preparation for the individual work that comes in the next step.

If you use writing with the children, this would be a time for written support.

Allow only a few minutes for this step (unless it is going very well) because children do not find story-making easy through dialogue alone—they need some action as well. This will be highlighted in the follow-up.

7 Each child in the circle now turns to a neighbour and begins a conversation with him or her, in the role of their own puppets.

8 Each pair of children now joins another pair and a conversation takes place between the four puppets.

9 All the children now walk about the room and meet each other's puppets.

10 Each child should now make a study of their puppet through drawing and writing. Give the children a suggested minimum number of items of information which you feel they are capable of writing.

They should do their final illustration and writing on the A3 paper so that it can be displayed and the puppet characters can be referred to in future lessons.

FOLLOW-UP 1

Having established the character of their puppets, it would be natural to use them again, perhaps in a play. Here are some storylines which you might give to the children:

- **A** loses something and **B** helps him/her to find it.
- **A** has something which **B** wants to have. What does **B** do? What does **A** do?
- **A** and **B** are in a frightening place. What happens? What do they do?
- **A** wants to do something. **B** does not want him/her to do it. What does **A** do? What does **B** do?
- **A** is hungry, but is fussy about food. **B** tries to find what food **A** would like to eat.

FOLLOW-UP 2

The puppets can write letters to each other.

VARIATION 1

Make specific puppets to link in with a story the children know, or which you are going to tell them.

VARIATION 2

Depending on the age of the children, they might be very happy to bring in their own teddy bears, dolls, toy dogs, etc., and to invent stories for them. They could teach their teddy bears English. But it is unwise to assume that they will be happy to give their teddy a name—some people keep their teddies for years and only ever refer to them as 'teddy'.

In any case, you can always bring an old teddy bear of your own to school. I have an old toy dog with one ear, and an old teddy bear with a hole in its throat because a man nailed it to a wall! He was a scrap merchant in Amsterdam and he nailed or tied any toy he found to the wooden and wire-netting walls of his yard. I found my teddy there one winter with snow on its head and chest, and rust running through the snow like blood. He sold it to me for 10p!

VARIATION 3

The puppets can be made from playdough and saltdough, which are two wonderful media—so easy to prepare, so adaptable, and so satisfying to use. If the puppets are approximately 10 cm high, or long, a town or village setting can be made for them at another time, and a soap-opera type of story can be based on them.

See the Appendix (page 139) for how to make your own playdough and saltdough.

COMMENTS

The youngest children will need a lot of help in making a puppet, and you may decide that it is better to use the simplest type, for example, a wooden spoon which they can draw on.

2.2 Masks

Masks release creativity, and a willingness in children to 'have a go' with the language. In the activity given here, I have suggested a range of things you can do, rather than concentrate on only one activity.

Here are suggestions for making human masks, animal masks, and fantasy masks. For dramatic reasons, it is probably better to have a balance between the different kinds of mask in the class as a whole.

I would suggest that all ages of children should begin with a paper plate into which you have put the two eye-holes.

Although four- and five-year-olds love masks, they normally cannot make complicated ones like the older children can. Encourage the older ones to use all the materials they can find to create unique characters.

LEVEL	**All**
AGE	**4–12**
AIMS	**Language:** to practise accuracy and/or fluency, depending on the activity you choose. Essentially, you can practise any language feature, grammar, or area of vocabulary you wish. **Other:** to use imagination to create masks with character.
TIME	**60–80 minutes**
MATERIALS	See Worksheets 2.2A and B for what you need for the masks. Paper plates, string, scissors, or a craft knife; video camera and tripod if available; mirror.
PREPARATION	Prepare a mask by following the instructions in Worksheets 2.2A and B (pages 148–9). Use the guiding marks given at the top of Worksheet 2.2A in order to mark where the eyes should be, and then cut the eyes out. The secret is to make a hole in the middle of the eye with the point of your scissors, make about six cuts from the hole to the edge of the eye hole, and then cut out the pieces. It is even easier if you use a craft knife.

IN CLASS

1 Show the children how to make a mask, using the paper-plate mask you have prepared as an example. Explain, preferably by demonstrating, how to make variations of hair, hats, etc. You might like to hand out copies of Worksheets 2.2A and B to groups of children, to give them ideas about what they might make. Give help where necessary, especially with cutting out the eye holes.

2 Tell the children about the character of your mask, then encourage them to think about who their masks represent, what their names might be, how old they are, etc. Get them to use whatever they have learnt to say in English. You might decide it is helpful if you write all the basic things they can say on the board.

3 When their masks are finished and fitted to their heads, the children can walk around the room talking to other children,

using the language you have written on the board. But to begin with, you might just tell the children to walk around, and say *Hello* to lots of other children.

You can control the conversations if you like. Here are some suggestions:

– Tell the children to walk round the room and to talk to at least five children, asking: *What's your name? How old are you?* You can then work through the basic question types they know.

– Write various times of the day on the board, for example, *7 o'clock, 8:30.* The children walk around, asking each other *What do you do at ...?* and answering *I usually ...*

– If the children know the phrase *You must ...,* ask them to make up three rules of behaviour. Tell them to wander round the room, wagging their fingers at other children, saying, *You must get up at five o'clock every morning/not play pop music/eat your vegetables).*

Use as many questions as you wish until the children have built up a sense of the individuality of their mask's character. Then give them a different situation, in which they can continue to use the same questions. Sit at the front, wearing a mask, and tell the class to ask you as many questions as they can. Don't wear a human mask—it's potentially disturbing for the children. You are very important to them! Wear a pleasant-looking animal mask, or a fantasy mask.

4 Ask the children to work in groups of four or five and make up a story. They should begin with a mime play, i.e. a play without words. They should perform their mime play for you (or for other groups), then write a simple narration and dialogue for the play, rehearse it, and perform it for the class.

Alternatively, you might prefer to write a story structure like this on the board:

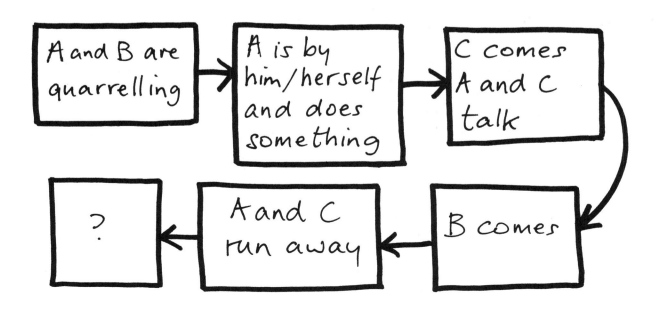

5 Once the children have performed their play, if you have a video camera you can record it on video (see 8.3).

VARIATION 1

Stand up

Ask the children to think about the character they have made, and to stand up and behave like him/her/it.

Teacher: *Stand up everybody who likes pop music/can ride a bicycle/has got a bicycle/has four legs/can fly/likes worms/is in love with a monster*, etc.

VARIATION 2

Interview

1 Tell the children that a visitor will come to the class. Put the children in pairs or groups, and ask them to prepare questions for the visitor which might be asked by the character their mask represents.

2 You go out of the room, put on a mask (and perhaps wearing a coat and scarf, carrying a bag, etc.), then come in and sit down. The children proceed to ask you questions.

VARIATION 3

Shopping

Show the children pictures of food and objects (or the clay food made in activity 1.4). Practise the names of the foods and objects, and give a price for them. Pairs write shopping lists on behalf of the characters that their masks represent, and based on the pictures you have shown the class. Give the pictures of food to the children who play the part of shopkeepers. One child from each pair tries to remember the shopping list and then, wearing his or her mask, goes shopping and tries to 'buy' all the things he or she remembers. The child returns to his or her partner, who checks if they have remembered to buy everything on their shopping lists:

Have you got…?
Yes, I have. No, I haven't.

VARIATION 4

Boasting

All the students mill about in the classroom, wearing their masks and boasting about what they did yesterday/last week/when they were one year old, etc.

VARIATION 5

Holidays

Taking their characters into account, the children discuss in groups where they want to go on holiday, and what they want to do. The children in each group try to agree on one holiday together which will let them all do whatever they want.

VARIATION 6

A party

The children plan a party: when, where, what games they might play, what music they might play, food, drink, decoration, invitations. They decide who is responsible for what. Then, of course, they hold the party, wearing their masks.

<table>
<tr><td>VARIATION 7</td><td>Diary
The children write the diary of one of the characters.</td></tr>
</table>

VARIATION 7

Diary
The children write the diary of one of the characters.

VARIATION 8

Letters
The children exchange letters: pen pals.

VARIATION 9

Describe and identify
Display all the masks on the classroom wall, or on tables. The children work in pairs. Child A thinks of one of the masks. Child B asks questions to find out which one it is.

FOLLOW-UP

Once the characters are established, the children can continue to use the masks in future lessons, playing out a 'soap opera' of individual incidents, dramas, and stories, and incorporating new topics, functions, and language as they are learnt.

2.3 Robots

Robot masks are particularly useful for imperatives, and for justifying repetition of simple language. Giving orders seems very natural when your head is inside a cardboard box!

LEVEL

All

AGE

4–12

AIMS

Language: to practise giving instructions.
Other: to make robot masks; to stimulate the children's acting abilities.

TIME

90 minutes to make the robots and to try them out.

MATERIALS

A piece of corrugated card or heavy wallpaper measuring 60 cm x 20 cm for each robot mask (alternatively, a cardboard box which is just big enough to fit on a child's head, or a paper bag), a craft knife, scissors, glue, sticky tape, silver foil, egg cartons, yoghurt cups, etc. for eyes, antennae, etc.

PREPARATION

Photocopy Worksheet 2.3 on page 150 for each individual or group, if you would like them to have reference copies.

IN CLASS

1 The children work on their masks, in pairs, groups, or individually, painting and sticking on eyes, antennae, etc. Give them the photocopied instructions if you wish.

2 Tell all the children who are dressed as robots that you are programming them. Use the language they know: *Stand up! Sit down! Stand up! Walk! Stop! Say hello! Sit down! Stand up! Go to the door! Open the door! Close the door! Go to your seat! Sit down!*

3 Teach the children (or revise): *Go forwards. Go backwards. Go to the right. Go to the left. Go slowly. Go quickly.*

Make a circle of children. Ask two robots to stand in the circle. Ask their two controllers to stand behind them. Tell the two controllers that they must not let their robot bump into the other robot. The controllers then tell their robots what to do, using the commands you have taught them. Other pairs can take over the roles.

<table>
<tr><td>FOLLOW-UP 1</td><td>

Story-making

You or a child describe what one or several children must perform: *You stand up. You walk along the path. You walk over the bridge. You walk up the hill. You walk down the hill. You walk through the swamp. You walk into the cave. You see the lion! You run!* etc.
</td></tr>
</table>

FOLLOW-UP 1

Story-making

You or a child describe what one or several children must perform: *You stand up. You walk along the path. You walk over the bridge. You walk up the hill. You walk down the hill. You walk through the swamp. You walk into the cave. You see the lion! You run!* etc.

FOLLOW-UP 2

Instruction manual

The children write a robot instruction manual, putting in all the things they want robots to be able to understand. They take turns to be the teacher robot, telling other robots what to do.

FOLLOW-UP 3

Robot rule

The robots make up rules for humans to obey. Then, in groups of four, they create science-fiction scenes to perform.

FOLLOW-UP 4

Human pets

1 In groups of three, Robot A talks to Robot B about his human pet, C. They then swap round. Each group creates a drama to perform for the other groups.

2 The robots write journals, letters and stories about their human pets. If the children want naturalism, they can do the writing from the captive humans' point of view rather than from that of the robots!

FOLLOW-UP 5

Display and storage

It would be a pity if the robot masks were to be spoilt. I suggest that you thread a strong piece of string through them all, and hang them across a wall.

2.4 Manikin

In this activity the children, as a class, help you to create a full-sized manikin of a man or woman, and begin to establish his or her character with the language they have. As they learn more language, so they invent more information about their manikin. This class character can become a key focus for the introduction and practice of language points in future lessons. The manikin can have a family, friends, job, home, hobbies, problems, hopes, joy, and sadness.

My experience is that young children do not automatically want to have an ordinary child as their pretend character—a princess is more likely. But many children like the character to be grown up, perhaps because they feel that he or she can do more things.

LEVEL	**All**
AGE	4–12
AIMS	**Language:** to practise describing people. **Other:** to use the imagination to make up a character; to make a full-sized human figure.
TIME	**60 minutes to make the manikin; 60 minutes to invent his or her character, and complete the drawing and writing.**
MATERIALS	Old clothes etc: trousers, shirt, socks, shoes; newspaper (or other material for stuffing, for example, foam rubber), thick card, felt pens, wool (for hair), glue, thin string, needles and thread, or a stapler.
PREPARATION	Cut a head shape out of the card.
IN CLASS	

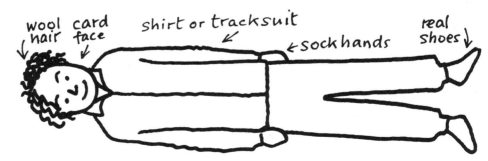

1 All the children contribute to making balls of old newspaper, then stuff them into the clothing.

2 You will have to roughly sew or staple the socks and the shirt to the trousers.

3 Begin by discussing with the children what sort of character they want. Either you or a child should then draw and cut out a face. Alternatively, a mask can be used, or a face can be drawn

onto a stuffed stocking. To begin with, you might show them what you have found for hair. Make holes in the neck, and fasten thin, tough string to the neck and shirt.

4 As you make the character, invite the class to use the language they have to invent characteristics for him or her—their name, age, job, home, birthday, etc.

5 Each child then draws the character in their own book, and writes down the characteristics established. (If you are going to spend a lot of time on these characters you might like to let the children have a separate book for their own character, and all the additional details and events of his or her life.)

You might also decide to make a large drawing with written details. This could be used as a wall poster.

VARIATION 1

A possible alternative is for each child to invent a character. However, young children probably gain far more from working together on the creation of one character. As time goes on, more characters can be invented: other family members (wife/husband and baby), neighbours (young and old), customers (if he or she is a shopkeeper), members of the social services (policeman, nurse), and pets.

VARIATION 2

Instead of starting with a person and developing a whole community, you can start with a pet—a cat, for example—and then add a family. Or you can start with a goblin or with a visitor from space.

2.5 Manikin's family

This activity follows on from the creation of the character described in 2.4, 'Manikin'.

LEVEL

Beginner and elementary

AGE

4–12

AIMS

Language: to practise describing people and family relationships.
Other: to learn to discuss and agree with other people (especially in the follow-up).

TIME

30 minutes to decide on the members of the family
20–30 minutes to make the 'photograph'
20–30 minutes for the family tree.

MATERIALS

A sheet of A5 paper, and another 6 cm x 10 cm sheet for each pair or group of three; two large sheets of paper (A1 or A2), one black and, if possible, one coloured; glue.

PREPARATION   If you are not familiar with family trees, practise drawing one before the lesson to see how it works.

IN CLASS

1 The class decide what sort of family the character has. The number of people in the family can be decided by the number of pairs or groups of children there are in the class with each responsible for one character.

2 Draw a family tree on the board, and encourage the children to base their suggestions on the structure of the tree.

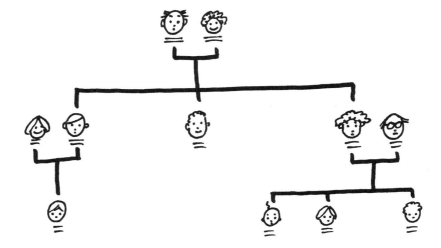

3 The class should discuss and agree on each character to become part of the family.

4 Each pair or group becomes responsible for making a picture of one family member on the A5 paper, cutting it out, and sticking it onto the black paper as part of a family 'photograph'.

5 Meanwhile, you can draw the family tree on another large piece of paper.

6 Each pair can also be asked to draw a much smaller portrait of the family member for whom they are responsible. This can then be stuck onto the family tree, named, and given a date of birth appropriate to the age of that person.

7 Each child makes a copy of the family tree in their book.

FOLLOW-UP   Once the family is established it can be used to provide the basis of any language practice. This could either be focused on specific language points, or more generally provide an opportunity and stimulus for creative use of the language they have acquired.

Here are some of the topics which might be developed through the family:

Discussing and designing a flat
Furnishing the flat
Deciding on and buying a pet
Problems in keeping a pet
Describing the person's hobby

Planning a picnic
Going on a picnic
Planning a party
Having the party
Christmas
Birthday
Being ill
Having an accident
Being burgled
Losing and looking for the pet
Planning and making a local history project.

3 Printing

The children's world is full of printed material: books, comics, papers, packets of food, and clothes. In the activities in this chapter, the children explore the effect of printing with different objects on different surfaces.

3.1 Rubbings

The children rub dark-coloured crayons on thin white paper which is pressed on an irregular surface, for example, a wooden floor. The resulting textures invite objective identification and, for children at elementary level and above, subjective interpretation.

LEVEL — **All**

AGE — 4–12

AIMS — **Language:** for the identification activity: *What is it? It's …*; for the interpretation activity: all the language at the children's command.
Other: to make 'rubbings' of objects on paper; to develop hand–eye co-ordination.

TIME — **30–40 minutes for the identification activity**
30–40 minutes for the interpretation activity

MATERIALS — For each pair of children: one A4 or A3 sheet of thin, white, or lightly-coloured paper, and some dark-coloured crayons or soft pencils.

PREPARATION — Make a rubbing of an object the children can identify and name in English, for example, a coin, the surface of an old table or chair, the sole of a shoe, the cover of a hardback book. If you have never done a rubbing before, just remember to keep the paper still, and make all your lines go in one direction.

Wood

Sandpaper

rope

IN CLASS

1   Show the children your rubbings, and ask them to identify them. (This is an example of when it is acceptable to say *What's this?*)
Teacher: *What's this?*
Child: *It's a table?*
Teacher: *A good idea, but no!*
Child: *It's the floor.*
Teacher: *Yes. Well done!*

2   Demonstrate how to make a rubbing. One or two children hold the paper on a surface. Rub the soft crayon or pencil across it, always in the same direction, in order to create consistent 'shadowing'.

3   Pairwork. The children make as many rubbings as they can in the classroom or (if allowed) elsewhere in the school.

4   The rubbings are exhibited, and the children take it in turns to ask questions:
Child: *Is it a desk?*
Child: *No.*
Child: *Is it a wall?*
Child: *Yes.*

VARIATION

The children can write down their identification, perhaps giving alternatives for other children to select from:
It's a wall.
It's a floor.
It's a table.

FOLLOW-UP

The children make a rubbing which produces irregular textures, and can be interpreted in a variety of ways. They then work out what they think the various shapes are, and tell other children about them. Writing can be used at this stage.

3.2   Printing vegetable poems

LEVEL

Beginners

AGE

4–12

AIMS

Language: to learn the vocabulary for vegetables, and make up poems. If you don't want the children to experience writing, let them create oral poems—children are masters of oral poetry!
Other: to learn about printing; making patterns and responding to them.

TIME   **40 minutes for the printing and 40 minutes for the poetry**

MATERIALS   As many vegetables as you can obtain (don't worry about what will print well and what will not—it is part of the children's learning to find out!); one A3 sheet of white or lightly-coloured paper for each child; a thin but opaque bag to put some of the vegetables in, so that the children can feel them through the bag; liquid paint, a vegetable knife, aprons, plastic sheets, water, and cloths; shallow containers such as plates—about three for each group of 4–5 children—each with a piece of sponge or foam rubber.

PREPARATION

1 Put a little liquid paint in each container.

2 Cut two or three vegetable cross-sections per child. You can cut the vegetables straight through, or at an angle, producing a more elongated shape. Here are some examples of basic shapes:

3 Practise printing with one or two vegetables so that you will be able to demonstrate with confidence. Press the cut surface of the vegetable into the sponge full of paint, and then press it onto the paper. Note that each loading of colour will produce more than one print, particularly if you print lightly.

4 Write out samples of poetry on a large sheet of paper:

Carrots and peas, please!
Carrots and peas?
Carrots and peas!
Carrots.
Peas.
Carrots and peas!
Carrots and peas!

IN CLASS

1   Help the children to enjoy the unusual sight of vegetables in the classroom! Show the vegetables, say the names for them, and drop them into the bag. Then challenge the children to feel the bag and identify the vegetables.

2   Praise the beauty of the vegetables, because that is what the whole lesson is about!

What a lovely carrot! I love its fat top and its thin little bottom! What a lovely vegetable!
Let's make pictures with these beautiful vegetables!

3   Put the children into groups of 4 or 5, and distribute the materials to each group.

4   Ask the children to draw two lines across their sheet of paper. Tell them that the two lines are paths which must join together. Show them two different ways of doing this (see the examples in the illustration).

5   Now tell the children to choose two vegetable shapes. They must print one of their vegetables carefully along the top path, then repeat with the other vegetable on the bottom path. Then they must decide what to do when the two paths meet: is it a happy meeting or an angry meeting? Be as open as possible to solutions and designs which do not coincide with your own idea of what is 'correct' or 'good'!

6   Once all the children have made their prints, have a display, and ask the children to talk about their pictures.

This is a carrot and this is a potato. They are walking along, then they meet and they become friends.
This is a cabbage and this is an onion. They are walking along, then they meet. They fight, and the cabbage wins. That is why there is no onion on the last bit of the path.

7   Now for the poetry! Children have a wonderful ear for word-play, and take great delight in it. The 'poetry' should revel in the sounds and rhythm of the words for vegetables, rather than

attempt the more sophisticated features of poetry. Rhythm, pace, alliteration, and similar sounds can all be focused upon. Read out the examples you have prepared. Emphasize the character of the words and phrases with your voice and body— this is very important—and get the children to copy you.

8 Once you feel that the children have got the idea of playing with the sounds, rhythms, and juxtapositions of the words, ask them to make up their own vegetable poems, and perform them for other children. Encourage them to touch the prints in their pictures with their fingers as they say their names.

VARIATION

The magic tree
1 Cut the vegetables as before, but with a greater variety of shapes, for example, a cross, a triangle, a square.
2 Ask the children to make a picture of a magical tree, using the different shapes.
3 Encourage the children to talk about the tree and its magical powers, and to create more pictures, for example, of animals and the mythical creatures that might live in the tree, or visit it.
4 Follow up with a writing activity, and display the children's pictures and texts on the walls.

3.3 Printing with everyday objects

In this activity, ordinary objects such as bottle tops and paper-clips are used for printing, and the children create pictures.

LEVEL

Elementary and above

AGE

5–12

AIMS

Language: to practise using *can* and the present simple tense; using *whose*.
Other: to develop awareness of the potential of everyday objects.

TIME

40 minutes

MATERIALS

An assortment of manufactured objects including, for example, rulers, wire, screws, hammers, coins, lids, bottle tops, paper-clips, coloured paints, shallow containers, pieces of sponge or foam rubber, one A3 sheet of paper for each pair of children, and one for you, aprons, plastic sheets, cloths and water. Copies of Worksheet 3.3, page 151.

PREPARATION

Fix a sheet of A3 paper on the board. Make one or two copies of Worksheet 3.3 (examples of machines) and pin them on the wall.

IN CLASS

1 Look at the collection of objects, and where possible name them.

Teacher: *What's this?*
Child: *It's a bottle top.*
Teacher: *What's this?*
Child: *It's a piece of wire.*

2 Ask 2 or 3 individuals to choose objects:

What do you want to try?

Ask them to experiment with the objects by first of all pressing them into a paint-loaded sponge, and then onto the paper on the board, so that all the class can see. Demonstrate the effect of overlapping and creating patterns with them.

3 Distribute the paper and objects. Ask the children to experiment with the objects for a few minutes on their own paper, making interesting patterns.

Teacher: *That's interesting/very nice/special*, etc.

Note: Remain open to fresh ideas, and encourage the children to be as experimental as possible. That may mean them doing things you don't expect, and inevitably their fingers and clothes will get inky or 'painty'! Encourage them to dab with their finger ends. If they want a subject, suggest a caterpillar, as this can be painted in any number of ways!

Show your excitement and delight in the variety and the thick and thin sensuality of the colours, and in the contrast of round and square, sharp and smudgy. Your excitement is of greater value than a hundred techniques!

4 Display all their experiments, and then tell the children that they are inventors. Say that you would like them all to design a machine which can do at least five special things. Discuss for a few minutes the sort of things the machines might be able to do. You might like to draw the children's attention to the examples on the wall.

5 The children now work in pairs on an A3 sheet of paper to create their machine. Encourage them to choose shapes, and create textures, which fit in with the machine they want to make.

At this point, you might want to show them the examples in the illustration.

Go round the classroom looking at the children's work, and ask about the five things the machines can do.

Teacher: *What can your machine do?*
    Can your machine do five things?
Child: *It can make an ice-cream. It can fly very fast. It can shout. It can show a video. It can brush a dog.*

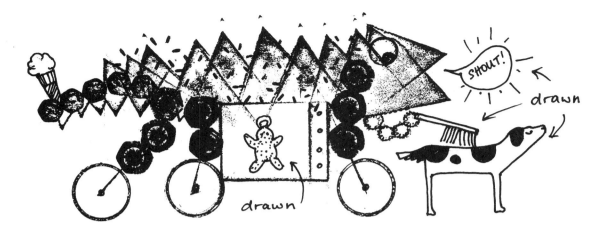

6 The children now write down, on an A5 piece of paper, the five things their machines can do.

7 Display all the machines with the inventors' names on. Display in a different location all the texts which have special titles instead of names, for example, *The ice-cream machine*. Make sure that each machine has a different title.

8 The children now try to match each picture with its title with the five things it can do.

Follow this up by questioning the children.

Teacher: *Whose is this machine?*
Child: *It's John's and Harry's.*
Teacher: *What can it do?*
Child: *It can jump over houses. It can fly to the moon. It can make sausage and chips. It can sing karaoke. It can swim.*

VARIATION 1

The children make a garden scene, printing with anything they can collect from nature: leaves, flowers, bark, twigs, stones. Encourage them to experiment to obtain the effect of different kinds of vegetation: forest, hedge, bush, grass, pond, etc. Make sure the children have some dark areas or clearly different colours, otherwise the whole effect will be too similar.

The children might like to add some wildlife, or some fairytale characters. Encourage them to talk about the creatures in their picture, and about their daily lives.

A goblin lives in the tree. Its baby is a little squirrel. The little squirrel hasn't got a mummy and a daddy. The goblin is its daddy now.

VARIATION 2

Fix the largest piece of paper you can find on the wall. A long frieze of black paper would be good. Make available one or two sources of thick paint or ink. Give each child at least five small pieces of plain paper, for example, 10 cm x 15 cm. The children then use any object they have to print with. If writing is allowed, they can write, for example: *This is my toe/finger/pencil/money.*

All the printings can then be displayed on the frieze.

4 Drawing by looking

Instead of looking carefully at nature as a rich source of visual inspiration, children often just look at each other's drawings. The result is that they tend to work with a very limited range of visual forms in their pictures, which often, for example, involve trees shown as round green blobs with brown sticks in the bottom.

Art is not only a form of emotional expression. As many of Leonardo da Vinci's drawings show, it also offers an opportunity for a cooler, more intellectual examination of experience. Leonardo remains a particularly good model for us, because his enquiries led him to make use of writing as well as drawing!

This chapter offers a collection of activities in which the children are encouraged to look, to study, to think and feel, and finally to communicate their understanding of what they see.

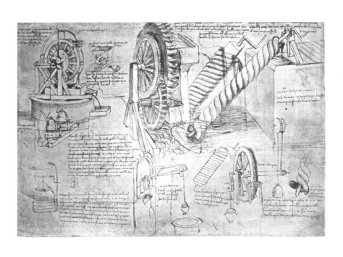 

Nobody can represent the total complexity of information contained in even the most modest of objects or settings. Artists who have drawn what they saw have always selected, and their selection has been partly influenced by the work of others. And just as it is impossible to do a picture of the 'whole truth', so it is impossible to be completely original in one's selection of what to paint. We are inevitably influenced by other paintings we have seen—even young children have seen literally millions of pictorial representations of things. So just leaving them to paint is a naive approach. We are more likely to help the child to develop if we offer a variety of thoughtful approaches to selecting from the infinite amount of information which fills our retinas.

Offering ways of seeing is not the same as offering tricks for drawing horses' heads, which is limiting to say the least. The ways of seeing proposed in this chapter are life enhancing rather than narrowing.

Language plays an important role in helping children to observe, and to make decisions: *Is it long or short? Is it fat or thin?*

4.1 Drawing by measuring: people

This activity offers a concrete experience of the proportions of the human body, and provides a basis for future observations of people in action.

Please note that the key proportions in adults are as follows: legs are approximately the same length as head and body together; upper and lower legs are the same length; upper arms are equal to lower arms (including the wrists and hands). In children, these proportions vary a little: the body and head together are longer than the legs.

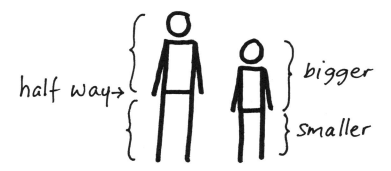

LEVEL	Elementary
AGE	5–12

Note: The five-year-olds will not be able to measure in the sense of using a ruler and reading the numbers. However, they will be able to use string to say if something is as long as something else.

AIMS	**Language:** *These are her legs. This is her arm*; and for the more proficient, height and length and approximation: *Her arms are about 50 cm. Her knees are about half way.* **Other:** measuring; to develop observation skills.

TIME	**30–40 minutes**

| MATERIALS | One or more large sheets of paper—white or pale-coloured wallpaper, for example, or paper from your local newspaper printer. The paper should be at least as large as a child, but if you are willing to be drawn, you will have to find a piece of paper long enough for you!
Coloured marker pens, a tape measure and rulers. |
|---|---|

IN CLASS

1 Clear a table, put a large piece of paper on it, and ask a child to lie on top of the paper. Ask different children to draw around the first child's body. Use the words referring to the body:

Mario, draw round Lucy's head! That's right, Mario is drawing round Lucy's head. Good.
Now, Judit, draw round Lucy's arm.

Alternatively, put a table against the wall and fix the paper above it. Ask the first child to stand on the table, and the second child to stand in front, in order to do the drawing. In this way the whole class can see the procedure.

Note: the children should try to keep their pens vertical.

2 Put the drawing on the wall. Write in the words for the parts of the body.

3 Ask different children to measure the different parts of the child's body on the drawing, and on his or her actual body. Use the word *about*.

Donald, how long are Melvin's legs? I see, about 60 centimetres. Good. Let's write it on the drawing.

4 Pairs of children take turns to measure each other and to write the measurements on a drawing in their books, taking up a full side of A4 paper. Ask questions such as, *Vivienne, how long are Timi's arms?* etc. in order to reinforce the vocabulary.

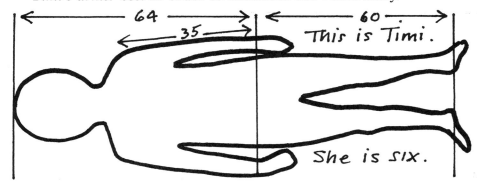

VARIATION 1

Have one piece of paper for each pair of children. Using two different coloured marker pens, the children take it in turns to draw around each other on the paper.

VARIATION 2

Using an overhead projector, for example, project a light at a child, and draw round the silhouette onto a large piece of paper.

VARIATION 3

Ask a child to draw round your own silhouette and measure different parts of your body. Use this information to begin to talk about the idea of basic adult proportions, and how children are different.

VARIATION 4

Use the activity to practise comparative forms.

Mary is taller than Tom.
Timi's body and head are longer than her legs.

FOLLOW-UP   A logical follow-up activity is to draw stick people (see 4.2).

4.2 Drawing stick people

Having learnt to look at the different proportions of people's bodies (see 4.1, 'Drawing by measuring people'), a next step is to look at how people move, and to draw different actions. The easiest way to do this is to reduce the drawing for each part of the body to a single line. In this way, the children can concentrate on proportions and actions.

Using 'sticks' for drawing is not a trick to save the children from having to think! They will have to think very hard, but only about one thing: the angle of the limb or body. The activity encourages them to look, think, and make decisions.

LEVEL   **Elementary**

AGE   **7–12**

AIMS   **Language:** to practise vocabulary for parts of the body, and language referring to size and shape; action verbs; the present continuous.
Other: to encourage careful observation.

TIME   **30–40 minutes**

MATERIALS   A large sheet of white or pale coloured paper, measuring about 100 x 150 cm; black paper strips about 3 cm wide: 3 for the body and legs, 65 cm long; 2 for the arms, 30 cm long; 2 for the feet, 20 cm long; a black disc of paper about 20 cm in diameter (for the head); two marker pens—one coloured and one black.

IN CLASS   1 Clear a table. Put a large piece of paper on the table (you might have to stick or tape it down). Ask one of the children to lie on their side on the table, as if they were running. Ask different children to draw around the different parts of the child's body. Use the words referring to the body:

Mario, draw round Lucy's head! That's right, Mario is drawing round Lucy's head. Good.
Now, George, draw round Lucy's arm.

Alternatively, fix the paper to the wall. Put a table against the wall. Ask the first child to stand on the table, and the second child to stand in front, in order to do the drawing. Then the whole class can see the procedure.

Note: the children should try to keep their pens vertical.

2 Put the drawing on the wall. Write in the parts of the body and what she is doing.

What's Julia doing? That's right, she's running.

Write *Julia is running* on the drawing.

3 Cut the black paper strips to the length of the body, the two halves of each leg, the feet and the arms. Hold them, or temporarily stick them, onto the parts in the drawing, and finish up with a stick drawing of the body on the body outline. The illustration is based on my daughter, Timi.

4 Talk about this. Let the children absorb the way in which the black sticks give the essence of the body in action. If you do writing with the children, write on the board:

The head and the body are as long as the legs.
The arms are half as long as the legs.

5 The children copy this running stick figure into their books. The drawings should be at least 20 cm in height. Try to get the children to copy the angles correctly. Basically, wide angles illustrate running quickly, and narrow angles illustrate running slowly. Also, make sure that they get the lines the right length: for a child, the head and body are just a bit longer than the legs. Ask:

Is it too long/short/wide/narrow?

6 Now that you have made a 'stick child', the children can experiment with other actions by rearranging the black strips on the drawing.

Child A: *What's she doing now?*
Child B: *She's walking/jumping/standing/skipping/falling/*
playing football, etc.

The children copy each of these actions into their books, and annotate them.

7 Brainstorm words for actions, and write them on the board. In groups of four or five, the children take it in turns to mime actions for the other children to identify.

Child A: *What am I doing?*
Child B: *You are running.*
Child A: *Yes, you're right.*

FOLLOW-UP

Having learned the principles of drawing stick people in action, the children might like to test their drawings on other children.

1 Give each child four small pieces of paper, for example, a piece of A4 paper cut into four pieces.

2 Ask the children to draw an action on one side of the paper and to write a sentence for the action on the other side of the paper, for example, *He's walking*.

3 The children should ask at least four other children:
Child A: *What's he/she doing?*
Child B: *He/she's walking.*

4 The children should give their sentences ticks (✓) if the other child guessed correctly what the actions showed, or crosses (✗) for the wrong action. Ask who got more ticks than crosses.

4.3 Drawing faces

In this activity the children learn to think about the proportions and shape of different people's faces. This general introduction to drawing faces is made more reflective in 4.4, 'Drawing your friend's face'. In the Variation, the children learn how to represent younger people. This provides a natural context for asking and talking about age.

LEVEL

Elementary and above

AGE

5–12

AIMS

Language: Describing facial features: face, hair, nose, eyes, eyebrows, mouth.
(Variation: *How old is he/she? I think he/she is about 5.*)
Other: hand–eye coordination; to observe proportion and shape.

TIME

40–50 minutes

MATERIALS

Pencils and erasers, a ruler about 40 cm long, a large sheet of paper.

PREPARATION

If you are unsure of your drawing ability, spend a little time drawing faces. It is easy if you follow the instructions below.

IN CLASS

1 Interest the class by drawing a smiling face on the board, and a speech bubble.

2 The face. Draw a large potato on your paper, at least 20 cm high.

Teacher: *What's this?*
Children: *It's a face.*

Ask the children to draw a similar face in their books. Call it a potato, to make the children relax, and feel confident that the circle does not need to be neatly drawn. It helps if you stipulate that their potato must be 10 cm high.

3 The eyes.

Teacher: *Now I'm going to draw the eyes.* (Pretend to begin to draw them, then stop and show you are not sure.) *Wait a minute! Where are the eyes?*

Demonstrate measuring faces and the position of the eyes on several students.

Teacher: *John ... your face is about 20 cm long ... and your eyes are about 10 cm from your chin. Oh! They are in the middle.*

Note:
a) Normally the eyes of adults are rather more than halfway up the face; children's eyes are lower.
b) Small, black dots represent rather hard, unfeeling eyes, larger dots look softer, and more sweet and innocent. You can tell the children this if you want to:

Teacher: *Small eyes are hard and angry. Big, soft eyes are warm and friendly.*

Now draw in the eyes.

4 The children measure their neighbour's face and position of the eyes. Go round the class asking questions about their findings.

The children now draw eyes into their potato faces ... about halfway up the face, or just below.

5 The nose. A small curved line is a useful representation of the nose for suggesting shape and position. It is about halfway between the eyes and the chin.

6 The children measure the position of each other's noses, then draw them in their books.

7 The mouth.

Teacher: *Let's have a happy mouth!* (Draw in the mouth.)

The children draw in mouths on their pictures.

8 The hair. Decide which of the children you measured you want to represent, and decide whether his or her hair is straight or curly, long or short. Draw the hair on your picture.

Teacher: *Who is this?*
Children: *It's Tom.*

The children draw the hair of their friend on their picture.

VARIATION

The children might like to know how to draw younger children. This is a very good topic for talking about age.

Draw three potatoes. Draw in the eyes on each one, placing them above the centre on the first one, below the centre on the next, and very near the bottom on the next.

Say: *How old is this man or woman? How old is this boy or girl? The eyes are high on men and women. The eyes are low on children. The eyes are very low on babies.*

Ask the children to do the same in their books.

Draw in strong eyebrows, and a strong nose and mouth on the grown-up. Draw in lighter versions on the child and on the baby.

Ask the children to do the same in their books.

Now you can add the text given in the illustration.

FOLLOW-UP 1

You can ask the children to look even more carefully by asking them to make a portrait of their friend.

You ask questions to help the children to learn to look, rather than drawing for them to copy.

First of all, ask the children to decide on the general shape of their friend's head, then move on to the other features:

> *Is his/her head round, square, long, thin, etc.?*
> *Has he/she got a small, pointed chin or a round chin?*
> *Are his/her eyes in the middle of his/her head or higher or lower?*
> *Are his/her eyes narrow or round?*
> *Is his/her hair curly, long, straight?*

Note: The *-ish* ending, representing approximation for adjectives, is very useful: *roundish, squarish, longish, thinnish*, etc.

FOLLOW-UP 2

If the children are interested, continue with: 4.4, 'Drawing expressions'; 5.5, 'Animal faces', and 5.6, 'Caricatures'.

COMMENTS

The suggestions given in this activity involve the children in looking carefully at faces. Although they are not tricks, they could easily become so. I suggest that you regularly remind the children to look at different faces, and think about their shapes and proportions.

4.4 Drawing expressions

The children learn to draw facial expressions. It is advisable to do 4.3, 'Drawing faces', before this activity. Facial expressions on their own are ambiguous: a person may look angry but actually be worried, for example. On the other hand, the activities given here are related to a universal experience of the way we use our faces to express emotions. It is important for the children to see that these are not tricks, but relate to observable phenomena. The follow-up activity will help to reinforce this idea.

LEVEL

Elementary and above

AGE

6–12

AIMS

Language: the vocabulary of shape and position; making comparisons; feelings.

Notes:

a) The comparative forms are listed here, but it is possible to do a modified form of the activity without the comparative forms.

b) I have given the examples with 'he' rather than 'she' because it is easier to omit drawing the hair, and a man can be bald! Obviously, you and the children can draw girls or women and draw in the hair.

TIME

40–50 minutes to do a selection of the expressions

MATERIALS

Large sheets of paper and markers for yourself.

PREPARATION

Practise drawing each of the expressions given here before the lesson, so that you feel confident you can do them in front of the children.

IN CLASS

1 Draw an angry face on the board.

Teacher: *How does he feel?*
Children: *He feels angry.*
Teacher: *Why is he angry?*
Children: *He's angry because a dog is eating his ice-cream/because he can't sleep.*

To help the children to invent more answers you can write these examples on the board:

He is angry because a dog is eating his ice-cream.
She is angry because he can't sleep.
He is angry because his daughter is silly.

2 Write the words *angry, happy, surprised, sad,* and *frightened* on the board (if the children are given writing). Ask them to work with a partner, and to take it in turns to mime the emotions, to see if the partner can recognize what it is that they are miming.

What comes out of this experiment is that there are certain characteristic positions, shapes, and angles of the features of the face which communicate these emotions. Drawing expressions must be based on these observable forms.

Tell the children that you are going to show them how to draw angry people and happy people.

Steps 3 to 8: Angry

3 Draw two potatoes on your paper. Ask the children to draw two potatoes, each one about 8 cm high.

Draw the eyes in the middle of the faces.

Draw the noses.

Ask the children to do the same in their books.

4 Ask a child with a face which creates expressions very easily, to act out anger … Show how his or her eyebrows come close together and close to the eyes. On the first face, draw the eyebrows straight and above the eyes. On the second face, draw the eyebrows touching the eyes, and touching each other in the middle.

He is angry. He is angrier!

5 Tell the children to copy what you have done very carefully. The language annotations on the illustration will make it easier for you to help the children.

6 On the first face, draw a short straight line for the mouth. Help the children to copy it.

   Make it straighter. Draw it lower/higher. Make it turn down. (Help them to understand, with a gesture.)

7 On the second face, draw a longer, turned-down line for an angrier mouth. Help the children to copy it.

   Make it longer. Draw it lower/higher. Turn down the corners.

8 Write underneath the first face: *He is angry.* Under the second, write: *He is angrier.*

Happy

9 Draw two potatoes on your paper. Ask the children to draw two potatoes, each one about 8 cm high.

   Draw the eyes in the middle of the faces.

   Draw the noses.

   Ask the children to do the same in their books.

10 Ask a child with a face which creates expressions very easily to act out being happy. Show how his or her eyebrows go up, and how the mouth curves up.

On the first face, draw the eyebrows curved, and just above the eyes. On the second face draw the eyebrows much higher, and more curved. Make sure there is a good space between the eyebrows, in order to show relaxed happiness.

11 Explain to the children that they should copy what you have done very carefully. Using the language annotations on the illustration will assist you in helping the children.

12 On the first face, draw a thin crescent moon for the mouth. Make sure the ends rise up. Help the children to copy it. Say:

Draw the corners higher (demonstrate).

13 On the second face, draw a half moon for the mouth. Make sure the corners turn up a bit. Help the children to copy it.

Make it bigger. Draw the corners higher.

14 Write underneath the first face: *She is happy.* Under the second, write: *She is happier.*

Note: make sure the mouths are not pulled down at the corners, because that could suggest misery, or even fear.

FOLLOW-UP

1 To help the children to appreciate that the expressions they have been drawing are based on life, and are not just cartoonists' tricks, you might do the following activity.

Put the children into pairs or small groups. List all the words for feelings on the board. As one half of the children take it in turns to act one of the feelings, the other half try to identify which those feelings are.

This activity can be followed up by the other children trying to guess why the child (acting the expression) is feeling that way.

2 Once the children can draw expressions on faces there are plenty of other things you can do! Here are some examples:
  - brainstorm lots of reasons why the person might be feeling like that
  - put two faces together, and imagine why they might be feeling like that, what they might be saying or thinking, what might be happening, what might have happened, and what might happen next
  - story making.

4.5 From geometric shapes to animals and birds

The sketchbooks of Villard de Honnecourt, who designed the first Gothic cathedral in England in the early 13th Century, contain drawings of creatures based on rectangles and triangles. This is an ancient technique and one which children can grasp and which helps them to grow in their appreciation of visual forms rather than merely equipping them with a trick.

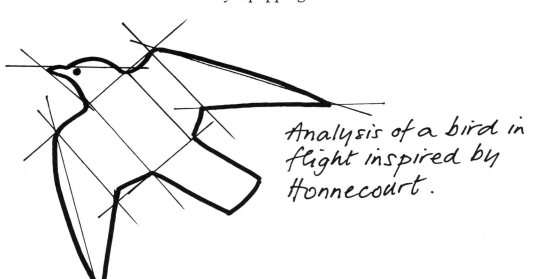

Analysis of a bird in flight inspired by Honnecourt.

In this activity the children are introduced to the idea and begin to apply it to drawing animals and birds. On Worksheet 4.5, page 152 you will find ten animals and birds based on geometric shapes. I suggest that you use three or four of them, at most.

This approach to drawing has great strengths, but there is a danger that the children will learn a different shape for each animal, and then not look at the actual animals again. The teacher should bear this in mind, and bring children back to regular observations of nature.

It is most important for the teacher to respect a child who has a completely different perception of the basic shape of an animal. In the example of a rabbit, given below, a useful starting point is to choose an oval, but arguments could also be put forward for a triangle or a rectangle!

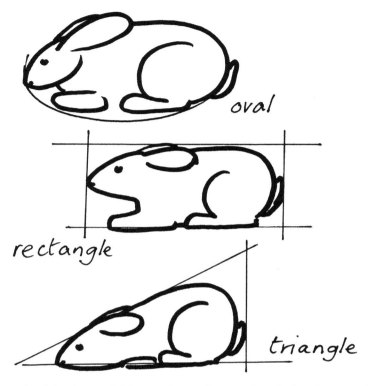

Of course, the ideal would be to have live animals in the classroom, so that the children could 'feel' their forms emotionally, and even physically. You might be able to do that with a rabbit or a turtle. Alternatively, you might like to make use of the many wonderfully naturalistic toy animals which are available these days. Their only disadvantage is that some of them are really very detailed, and there might be too much for the children to cope with in drawing them.

LEVEL	**Elementary and above**
AGE	**7–12**
AIMS	**Language:** vocabulary for geometric shapes (*rectangle*, *square*, *triangle*, *circle*, *oval*), animals and parts of animals. **Other:** hand–eye co-ordination; to learn to draw animals.
TIME	**40–50 minutes**
MATERIALS	A copy for each child and for you of the pictures on Worksheet 4.5 (page 152) of the animals you want to draw. Paper and pens/pencils.

PREPARATION

Study the pictures beforehand, and think about the basic shapes involved.

IN CLASS

1 Revise the words for shapes learnt in earlier activities. Draw the basic geometrical shapes in the air with your finger (invisible drawings!). Ask *What's this?* If their memories need help, ask them *Is it a rectangle, a square, a triangle, a circle, or an oval?*

2 Tell them: *Today we are going to draw a lot of animals.* Let the children brainstorm the words they know for animals.

3 Give them copies of Worksheet 4.5 about animals. Choose one of the animals, and draw its basic geometrical shape in the air with your finger. Ask the children to say which one it is. It is advisable to choose an extreme shape of animal to draw invisibly, for example, an elephant (big and rather square), or a crocodile (a long rectangle), or a rabbit (oval head, oval body, two long, thin oval ears).

Teacher: *What's this?*
Children: *It's an elephant.*

Redraw the elephant in the air, bit by bit.

Teacher: *What's this?*
Children: *The elephant's back/body.*
Teacher: *What's this?*
Children: *Its head/ear/trunk/legs.*

4 Continue to raise awareness of the way each animal has a basic shape, and the proportions of that shape (for example, a short, fat oval, or a long, thin oval). Draw basic shapes of animals in the air, either with invisible drawing, or on the board. For example, draw a square and draw a long thin rectangle.

Teacher: *I'm going to draw a crocodile and I'm going to draw an elephant.* Draw a long thin rectangle. *Is this the elephant or is this the crocodile?*
Children: *It's the crocodile.*

Repeat this technique with other animals, practising the animals' names, and making the children familiar with the idea that they really can recognize animals by their basic shapes (particularly if you make the choices quite extreme).

5 Begin to draw the animals one by one. This example is based on a drawing of a rabbit.

Teacher: *We are going to draw a rabbit. Is it a rabbit: a rectangle, a triangle, a circle, or an oval?*
Children: *It's an oval.*

Draw an oval on the board. Ask the children to draw an oval in their books. You might need to say: *Good. Make it thinner/fatter/longer/shorter/bigger.*

It is important to get the proportion of the basic shape right, as well as the general choice of shape.

Teacher: *We are going to draw the rabbit's head. Is a rabbit's head: a rectangle, a triangle, a circle, or an oval?*
Children: *An oval.*

Now the ears.

Teacher: *We are going to draw the ears. Are they: squares, rectangles, triangles, circles, or ovals?*
Children: *Ovals.*
Teacher: *Are they long, thin ovals, or short, fat ovals?*
Children: *Long and thin.*

Draw two long, thin ovals for the ears.

FOLLOW-UP

The most obvious follow-up is to make use of this ancient technique in making further drawings. The principle does not just apply to animals, but to any object whatsoever. If the children enjoy this activity it would be worth asking them to add details of information about the animal: where it lives, what it eats, and so on.

4.6 Houses

This activity deals directly with the tendency of children to build up a fixed and very simple 'drawing vocabulary'. Just as we all use the word *house*, so most children draw more or less the same picture of a house. And just as we help the children to widen their vocabulary, to be able to tell us more about the house, we must also help them to widen their 'picture' vocabulary, so they can tell us about the particular house they want to draw. We must continually stretch and open their understanding of art as a way of exploring.

LEVEL

Elementary and above

AGE

5–12

AIMS

Language: adjectives to describe architectural features.
Other: hand–eye co-ordination; to make the children aware of the variations in styles of houses.

TIME

50 minutes

MATERIALS

For each child: Coloured pens or pencils, an ordinary black pencil, one A5 and one A4 sheet of paper, scissors.

For the teacher: paper to make a frieze about 50 cm deep, and long enough to allow 15 cm for each child's picture.

PREPARATION

Prepare the paper for the frieze and put it on the walls before the lesson.

IN CLASS

1 Give each child a piece of A5 paper. Make sure that each of them places the paper vertically, and has an ordinary black pencil to draw with. Challenge the children to draw a house in ten seconds. Count to ten, slowly, as the children draw. At the end of ten seconds, ask the children to stop and to write their names on the back of the paper.

2 Collect the drawings, mix them together, display them, and then challenge the children (perhaps in threes) to identify their own drawing.

Teacher: *Rita, George, and Yoshima, come here. Now where is your house, Rita? Is that yours? Are you sure?*
It's difficult, isn't it? They are very similar!
Oh, yes. That's yours! It's special! The house is very tall, and it has a lot of windows.

Your aim is to help the children to realize that if a house is special, it is easy to recognize.

3 If there is a view of different kinds of houses from your classroom window, or if it is possible to go for a walk to see different kinds of houses, please do so! Ask questions so that the children have to look carefully. However, don't expect them to be able to say very much—it is not so easy to describe a house in words!

Teacher: *Tell me about the yellow house.*
Children: *It is big/small/high/low. It has a pointed roof/a flat roof. There are two windows, and there is a door.*
Teacher: *Are the windows square, pointed, or round?*
Children: *They are round.*

This would be a wonderful achievement! The main thing is that they should look at the different forms of houses, become more aware of, and see how they differ from the pictures they normally do.

4 Return to the classroom. Each child should have a piece of A4 paper. Tell them that they each have to draw a special house. Tell them that you will help them with questions, but they must decide what their invented house is like—it must be unique! Here are some of the questions you can ask (remember that you can mime every one of these adjectives, so the vocabulary should not be too difficult):

Is your house big or small? Is it tall or small? Is it wide or narrow? Has it got a pointed roof or a flat roof? How many windows has it got? How many doors has it got? Are they big or small?

As you ask these questions, get some of the children to say what their house is like. The aim is to help them to create a unique house.

5 The children should now draw their houses in pencil.

6 The children should walk about the classroom to make sure that their house is special, and not like other children's houses.

They can return to their places and change their drawings if they wish. Tell them to add at least one interesting-looking person and animal looking out of one of the windows.

7 Finally, they should colour their houses and then cut them out.

8 Stick each child's house on the upper side of the frieze. The middle is a street, and the side opposite the houses is a park, with grass, paths, ponds, trees, etc.

Sketch of part of a long frieze. The houses, cars, trees, etc. painted by the children, cut out, and stuck down on to the frieze. The clouds, road, path, grass, etc. can be painted on the frieze or stuck on.

9 The houses and the street can provide a good setting for a 'soap' community. See also 1.9, 'Town and country setting'.

VARIATION 1

The children can take it in turns to describe a house in the street so that another child can identify it.

VARIATION 2

Instead of all the children drawing a house, two or three houses could be created by the class as a whole, through discussion. That would make it easier for the very young.

5 Drawing from imagination

We must encourage our children to look inside themselves as well as outside; drawing from imagination is vital for the children's growth. But, just as we must help the children to learn to look harder and harder at the world around them, we must also encourage them to look imaginatively beyond the first images that are lying around in their minds which are, so often, well-known images picked up from other children.

5.1 My head

The children draw large profiles of each other's heads, and then draw pictures inside the heads which illustrate aspects of their lives, ranging from their family to their fears.

LEVEL	**Elementary and upwards**
AGE	**4–12**
AIMS	**Language:** talking about oneself; home and family, possessions, desires, difficulties. **Other:** to think about one's feelings.
TIME	**40–50 minutes minimum**
MATERIALS	A light of some kind to help produce a shadow—it could be an overhead projector, a table lamp, or even a torch; an A3 sheet of plain paper and scissors for each child; one A3 sheet of paper for you; glue; magazines, comics, and other publications with lots of small pictures which could relate to the children's interests and concerns.
PREPARATION	Cut out or draw some pictures beforehand to represent aspects of your life—your interests, things you are scared of, and so on.
IN CLASS	1 Setting up the light will engage the interest of the children. Don't tell them what you are doing, in order to hold their attention. Fix a sheet of paper on the wall for the shadow to fall on.
	2 Ask a child to sit so that the shadow of his or her head falls on the paper.

3 Ask another child to draw around the shadow.

4 Put up another sheet of paper, and ask a child to draw around the shadow of your head. Then stick the pictures you have prepared inside the profile, explaining their significance as you do so.

5 Brainstorm with the children the sort of things they might like to put inside their own profiles, bearing in mind that they should be able to talk about what they have illustrated.

At a low proficiency level: home, family, pets, possessions.

At a higher level: what they think is beautiful or ugly, their joys, fears, desires, criticisms.

6 Now let the children work in pairs and draw around each other's shadows. As only two children can work on this at a time, let them start drawing pictures and/or cutting out pictures from magazines which illustrate their interests and concerns. When they have had their profiles drawn, they can stick the pictures inside.

7 The children show others their profiles. They try to guess what each of the other children is trying to represent.

5.2 A poster of things

The children illustrate as many of the nouns they know as they can. They then stick them on a large poster. The effect of the brightly coloured objects, cut out and glued onto a white or black background, is very attractive.

LEVEL — **All** (Beginners only need 20 or so nouns to be able to do this.)

AGE — 5–12

AIMS — **Language:** to talk about possession, practise using the definite and indefinite articles, and describing things and people.
Other: to co-operate as a class to make a poster.

TIME — **40 minutes to get the poster started. It can be continued in later lessons**

MATERIALS — The largest piece of paper you can find (or make, by sticking smaller pieces together), glue, three or four pieces of paper measuring 10 cm x 15 cm, and a pencil for each child; coloured pencils or paints.

PREPARATION — Draw and colour one picture representing an English word they know.

IN CLASS — 1 Show the children the big piece of paper you have prepared. Put it up on the wall. Show the children the picture you have prepared. Ask them what it is, and what they can say about it. Glue it on the poster.

2 Brainstorm all the words the children can think of which can be illustrated by them. If you use writing, write their ideas on the board.

3 Agree with the children on who illustrates each of the words. In order to make sure that you can focus their minds on the use of the articles *a*/*the*, make sure that: (i) there are several examples of the same object, but coloured differently, or with some other feature which makes it individual (*the*); and (ii) there are several objects which are identical (*a*). Make sure that each picture is no bigger than 5 to 7 cm across.

4 As the children finish their pictures, tell them to cut them out, then help them to stick them on to the large poster.

FOLLOW-UP

Once there are about 100 objects on the poster, it becomes a genuine challenge to answer such questions as:

Where's the red ball. (i.e. there is only one)
Where's a green bird (i.e. there are several)
Where's Wendy's cat? Where's Tim's monster?
Child A: *I'm thinking of something green.* Child B: *Is it a green monster?*
Child A: *How many sad faces are there?* Child B: *There are three*, and so on.

5.3 Amazing invention

The children invent an amazing machine. They label its parts and explain—orally and/or in writing—how it works.

LEVEL

Elementary and above

AGE

8–12

AIMS

Language: to use the present simple to describe how the machine works.
Other: to use their powers of invention.

TIME

2 hours

MATERIALS

For each child: an A4 photocopy of the picture of an amazing machine invented by a boy of nine and described by him (see Worksheet 5.3, page 153), an A4 sheet of plain paper.

One A3 copy of the invention for you.

PREPARATION

Try to arrange for the children's inventions to be displayed somewhere outside of the school, such as the reception area of a local factory, or in the local library.

IN CLASS

1 Show the children the 'dog exercising machine' drawing by Kristof Orzoy, aged 9. Discuss what it does for the dog.

2 Ask the children to brainstorm on the board other machines that would be very useful to invent. Here are some examples to set your own mind going!

A machine to:

exercise a pet fish
exercise a pet hamster
boil an egg and put it on the table
stop burglars getting into the house
make you laugh
protect you from bullies

3 Ask pairs of children to decide which of the machines they would like to work on. Tell them they are going to draw it. If you want them to include written explanations, ask them to fold one third of the paper back, and to draw on the remaining two thirds (the one third is for the explanatory text). Fine pens should be used to encourage a feeling of 'machine-like precision', but rulers should not be used, because then the standard sought after will be too high, and the children will be disillusioned: wobbly lines are OK if they're drawn with a fine pen!

4 The children design and draw. You circulate, asking questions and making statements. For example:

What are you designing/drawing?
Which machine are you designing/drawing?
How does it work?
What happens?
I like it very much. It's a really good idea!
Tell me about it.
That's very nice/interesting/great/wonderful!

5 When the drawings are finished, ask the children to add a numbered label to each part they want to explain, and then to draft their explanatory sentences. You will have to help them at this time because they are unlikely to have all the words they need. You will find quite a few useful words and phrases on Kristof Orzoy's drawing.

6 When the children have drafted their explanatory sentences, and corrected them with your help, ask them to write the sentences on the paper, below the drawing on the lower third of the sheet. If necessary, help the children to add an extra strip of paper for longer texts.

7 Display the inventions in the classroom. Ask one child from each pair to stand next to his or her invention in order to talk about it. Ask the other child from each pair to go round looking at other children's inventions, and asking questions. After ten minutes or so, they can change over.

8 Finally, display the inventions in whatever location outside the school that you have been able to arrange.

5.4   Blind dictation

This activity makes the children think about the shapes of things they know while they are drawing, without the support of their visual sense.

LEVEL

Beginners and upwards

AGE

5–12

AIMS

Language: parts of the body.
Other: to draw an animal, using all of the senses except sight.

TIME

30 minutes

MATERIALS

For each child: a blindfold, paper, and pens.

PREPARATION

Find a photograph of something you would like the children to draw, preferably from its most characteristic viewpoint, for example, an elephant seen from the side.

IN CLASS

1 Ask the class to tell you everything they can about elephants.

Teacher: *Tell me about elephants! Are they big or small?*
Child A: *They are big.*
Child B: *They are strong.*
Child C: *They live in Africa and India.*
Child D: *They have big legs and big ears and little eyes and a little tail.*

2 Show the class the picture of an elephant. Confirm that the children were right in their descriptions. In this way, you can revise or teach the language for parts of the body, as well as helping the children to visualize the shape of the elephant.

3 Give each child a piece of paper and make sure they each have a pen.

4 Now begin to put the blindfolds on them! This should be the first time that they realize that they are going to be blindfolded.

5 Tell the children to feel their paper and their pen.

Teacher: *Can you feel your paper … and your pen? Now, hold your pen. Now put your pen on the left-hand side of the paper, and draw a long trunk. Now draw the top of the elephant's head. Now draw the elephant's back. Now draw the elephant's back leg. Now draw the elephant's front leg. Now draw the elephant's mouth. Now draw the elephant's ear. Now draw the elephant's eye. Now draw the elephant's tusk.*

6 Tell them to take off their blindfolds. They look at their own and each other's pictures.

7 Put them in pairs, A and B. A and B look at A's picture. B points at each part of the body on A's picture as you say the word for it.

Teacher: *Point to the head and to the tail. Say what they are.*
Child: *This is the head and this is the tail.* (Make sure that B gives a full sentence, and uses the key word rather than merely pointing.)

8 Now the pairs look at B's picture and repeat the procedure.

9 Each child should annotate his or her drawing, naming each part of the body.

FOLLOW-UP

Exhibit all the drawings.

5.5 Animal faces

This activity should only be done when 4.3, 'Drawing faces', and 4.4, 'Drawing expressions', have been done.

Children clearly love the idea that animals can experience the same feelings as people. To be able to draw these feelings opens up many opportunities for imaginative work.

LEVEL

Elementary and above

AGE

6–12 years

AIMS

Language: to practise vocabulary for shapes of faces, and for facial features and their appearance.
Other: to think about feelings and how they show on our faces.

TIME

30 minutes

MATERIALS

3 large sheets of plain paper and a marker pen, a teddy bear or other toy animal.

PREPARATION

Make sure you are confident that you can draw the animal by doing a bit of practice before the lesson.

IN CLASS

1 Introduce your animal. Talk to the children about it, asking questions, making statements, and gradually building up a picture of it on the board.

Teacher: *Sometimes my teddy bear is sad. Look!* (Draw a circle plus two smaller circles for ears.) *What's this?*
Children: *Your teddy bear.*
Teacher: (drawing the eyes) *What are these?*
Children: *They are eyes.*
Teacher: (drawing the nose) *What's this?*

Children: *A nose.*
Teacher: (drawing the mouth turned down) *What's this?*
Children: *A mouth.*
Teacher: *Is he sad or is he happy?*
Children: *He's sad.*
Teacher: *Why is he sad, do you think?*
Children: *I think he's sad because he can't find his mummy.*

2 Using the examples of animal faces given here, you can now help the children to draw more of them, with various expressions. Revise adjectives as you guide them, for example:

Has it got a round head or an oval head? Is its tail long or short?

oval

circle   circle   circle

3 They can also write a few sentences under each drawing:

This is a lion. He/she is sad/happy because ...

FOLLOW-UP

Once the children can draw animal faces, they can invent stories, dialogues, and daily routines for them.

5.6 Caricatures

Children love caricatures, and long to be able to invent and draw cartoon characters. We tend to look down on such an interest, forgetting that Leonardo da Vinci himself found it worthwhile and, indeed, fascinating.

LEVEL

Elementary and above

AGE

6–12

AIMS

Language: to practise vocabulary for the shapes of faces, facial features, and their appearance.
Other: to learn to draw cartoon characters.

TIME

40–50 minutes

MATERIALS

2 large sheets of plain paper and a thick felt-marker.

IN CLASS

1 In this first step we suggest that you continue to pretend that you are going to draw, but then stop, turn to the class, and ask the children for guidance. If you follow this same procedure

throughout the introduction, the children will love it. You can teach new language by giving alternatives, and by using mime, drawing in the air, etc.

Teacher: (pretending you are about to draw, and then stopping) *Do you want a man, a woman, a boy, or a girl?*

Children: *A girl.* (If they ask for a boy and a girl, draw both, it will be even better language practice for them.)

Teacher: (pretending you are about to draw, and then stopping) *Has she got a round face, an oval face, a square face, or a triangular face?*

Children: *A triangular face.*

Teacher: (pretending you are about to draw, and then stopping) *Is it a big triangle or a little triangle?*

Children: *Big!*

Now draw a big triangle on the board. Invite the children to do the same in their books. Their triangle should be at least 10 cm high.

Now for the eyes.

Teacher: (pretending you are about to draw and then stopping) *Has she got little eyes or big eyes?*

Children: *Big eyes!*

Teacher: (pretending you are about to draw and then stopping) *Are they at the top of her head or in the middle of her head?*

Children: *At the top of her head!*

Teacher: (Draw the big eyes at the top of her head) *Now, the nose!*

Teacher: (pretending you are about to draw and then stopping) *Has she got a big nose or a little nose?*

Children: *Big nose!*

Teacher: (pretending you are about to draw and then stopping) *Is it a big, fat nose or a big, thin nose?*

Children: *A big, fat nose!*

Teacher: (Draw the big, fat nose)

Continue in this way until the character has all her features.

2 Encourage the class to invent a lot of things about the girl they have created. Take into account that the children have created a caricature, so encourage extreme ideas. *She's 115 years old. Her name is Peter! She collects old socks.*

Either continue to develop the character of the person the children have created, or help them to draw their own version in their books, making use of the same language.

If you feel it is appropriate, it would be natural to use comparative forms when helping the children.

Teacher: *Draw it longer/fatter/bigger*, etc.

3 In this step you help the children to invent their own individual character. The children might like to work in pairs.

Teacher (drawing a circle, an oval, a square, and a triangle):
Now you can make a person. Has he or she got a round face, an oval face, a square face, or a triangular face?

(The children choose the shape they want to use, and draw it in their books.)

round   oval   square   triangular   square
                                                                 and
                                                                 triangular

4 The children now invent special information about their character. You can guide the description with questions written on the board:

What's his/her name?
How old is he/she?
What are his/her hobbies?
What is his/her favourite food?

5 The children can now walk about the classroom, introducing their character to other children, or to other invented characters. They can ask for information by using the same questions you have written on the board.

FOLLOW-UP

The characters the children have made could become the basis for a soap opera created by the class, and for future story-making. Apart from the more obvious imaginative activities, the invented characters can also be used, for example, to illustrate and practise more mundane language and ideas of daily routines.

5.7   Who is he?

The children speculate about what might be happening in an ambiguous picture. You could also invite the children to speculate on what has happened, and what will happen. It is helpful if the children have done 4.2, 'Drawing stick people', before trying this one.

LEVEL	**Elementary and above**
AGE	4–12
AIMS	**Language:** Questions; descriptions of people. **Other:** to practise speculating.
TIME	**20 minutes**
MATERIALS	A large sheet of paper (about 50 cm x 100 cm).
PREPARATION	Draw one of the pictures below on the paper.

IN CLASS

1 Show the picture to the class.

2 Ask the children various questions about the picture. For example:

How many people are there in the picture?
Are they men or women, boys or girls?
How old is he/she?
Where are they?
What are they doing?
Why are they running?
What is he/she saying/thinking/feeling?
What's this? Is it a box or a window? What is it?
Gather the children's ideas, and build up a description of the picture.

3 Write the descriptive sentences below the picture and display it.

FOLLOW-UP

Each child draws an ambiguous picture and prepares at least ten questions about the picture. Each child then shows the picture to at least two other children in turn, and asks them the questions. The children write down their preferred answers under their pictures, and display them.

VARIATION

If the children know the present perfect and future tense forms you can give them an opportunity to use these tenses by extending the questions.

Teacher: *What has just happened? What has he done? What will he do next?*

5.8 House of the thin woman

In this activity, you demonstrate to the children that their memories and imaginations contain an enormous range of visual images and they do not need to restrict themselves to drawing the same limited range of pictures all the time.

LEVEL

Elementary and above

AGE

5–12

AIMS

Language: to develop listening skills.
Other: to learn to draw on the store of images in their memories.

TIME

60 minutes

MATERIALS

For each child: two A4 sheets of plain paper, coloured pens or pencils.

PREPARATION

Write two descriptions, one very simple and one with details, to read to the children so that they can draw what you describe. (If you prefer, you can use the examples in the instructions for the activity.)

IN CLASS

1 Tell the children that you want them all to draw the picture you describe. Then describe a picture very simply, without giving any details about the various items in it. For example:

In your picture there must be two houses, three clouds, and a woman.

Give the children 15 minutes to do the picture.

2 While the children are doing the picture, go round and make helpful suggestions on their work. Introduce the idea of giving value to pictures which are special: *That's a very special house!*

3 Display the pictures. Let the children see them for a few minutes. Mildly comment on the similarity of ways of drawing many of the things. Praise special, individual representations of the objects given.

4 Now ask the children to tidy their desks and to get their second piece of paper ready. Tell them that you will describe another picture which you want them to draw. Explain that they must first of all just sit and listen to your description of the whole picture, and then you will help them bit by bit. They can close their eyes if they want to.

For this picture you will give much more detail. For example:

The house is very tall. It is wide at the top and thin at the bottom. At the bottom there is one door. There are no windows. In the middle of the house, there are three windows and at the top of the house there are five windows. The roof is a tall triangle and on the top of it there is a ball. The house is standing on the top of a hill.

Now tell the children you will read the description again and they must draw what you describe with a soft black pencil. The paper can be vertical or horizontal. Make sure that the children follow the description you give, but don't interfere with their interpretation of it. For example, don't demand that they place the paper vertically and have the hill just at the bottom of the paper – that is their business! Your main purpose is to help the children to really emphasize what it is that they want to show.

Rita! Is that a tall house? Draw it very, very tall!
Bill! Is your house thin at the bottom? No! Draw it very thin at the bottom!

5 Let the children walk about and look at each other's pictures.

6 Tell them to return to their places and get their crayons or pens ready. Then they must listen. Tell them this:

A very tall woman lives in your house. Some people say she is very nice and some people say she is not very nice. You decide. She is very tall and very thin. Draw her next to the house.

Let the children draw her. Then say:

Is your thin woman nice or not nice?
Now, if you think she is very nice, make her clothes beautiful colours. But if you think she is not very nice, make her clothes unpleasant colours.

7 Next the children must colour the house.

You: *If your thin woman is not very nice then draw not very nice colours on the house. If she is nice then draw nice colours on her house.*

8 Now the children must colour the sky and the hill.

You: *Is your woman not very nice? Then draw the sky with dark/black clouds at the top and behind the house. Is she nice? Then draw the sky with a happy colour at the top and behind the house.*

9 Display all the pictures. Half of the children should stand by their pictures and half can walk about and comment.

Child A: *That's a nice picture! I like the house/woman/sky. It's very special!*
Child B: *Thank you.*

6 Colours

The range of colours we can perceive is infinite. This complexity is overwhelming, and it is not surprising that children, learning from each other, build up a very simple range of colours to describe the world around them. Trunks are brown and leaves are green!

This wish to simplify in order to understand easily is typical of us all. Our job as teachers is to help children to remain curious, to continually look and reflect, and remain open to new understandings.

This section has activities designed to encourage children to study the variety of colours in nature, and activities which are more to do with the way colours relate to each other in a painting.

6.1 Primary, secondary, and tertiary colours

This activity focuses on two key points about colour:

1 That two primary colours mixed together make a secondary colour which is also a complementary colour ('complementary' in this case means that they enhance each other, and look good together).

2 That colours can be mixed to produce an enormous variety of different colours, as well as different shades of the same colour.

LEVEL	**Elementary**
AGE	**4–12**
AIMS	**Language:** to practise the vocabulary of colours. **Other:** to learn how to mix colours.
TIME	**40 minutes**
MATERIALS	Red, blue, and yellow chalks/coloured pens/felt pens/paints.
PREPARATION	Try the colours you have found to make sure they produce the right secondary colours: red + yellow = orange, red + blue = purple, blue + yellow = green.
IN CLASS	1 Draw three rectangles like this:

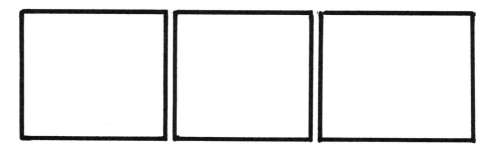

Hold up the red pen.

Teacher: *What colour is this pen?*
Child: *It's red.*

Now fill in the first rectangle on the board with the red pen.

2 Hold up the yellow pen.

Teacher: *What colour is this pen?*
Child: *It's yellow.*

Now fill in the third rectangle with the yellow pen.

3 Hold up both pens.

Teacher: *What do red and yellow make?*
Child: *Orange.*
Teacher: *Let's see!*

Pretend that it is rather like magic! Make some drama out of it!

Teacher: *John, come and draw yellow in this middle square.*
  Anna, come and draw red on the yellow.
  Ha! Haaa! Orange!

4 Write the colours under the squares.

5 Repeat steps 1 to 4 to show that red and blue make purple, and blue and yellow make green.

6 Now write the sentences:

Red and yellow make orange.
Red and blue make purple.
Blue and yellow make green.

7 Give the children a copy of the 'chart' and ask them to fill in the colours as you have done, write the words and sentences next to the right squares, and then put the chart in their books.

8 Now you can challenge children to make colours on the board.

Teacher: *Can you make orange?*
Child: *Yes.*
Teacher: *What colours do you want?*
Child: *Red and yellow, please.*

Give the child the colours, and congratulate him or her.

9 Individual children can now challenge other children.

10 Now show the children how brown can be created from a mixture of all three primary colours. Ask them to complete their chart with the same effect.

FOLLOW-UP 1

The children are touching on a very interesting area in art: colour mixing. They will find, even in this simple experiment, that some primaries are better than others for making secondary colours. This invites experimentation, so that the child becomes familiar with what makes a good green, or orange, or purple and what produces a very dull result. Hence the sentences:

This yellow and this red make a lovely orange.
This yellow and this red make a dull orange.

Furthermore, in describing colours, it is very helpful to be able to suggest that the colour is not 'pure'.

This is a yellowy orange.
This is a bluey green.
This is an orangey red. Really, it's orange!

FOLLOW-UP 2

Another way to experience how colours mix is to create a new colour by cutting a white cardboard disc, colouring half of it yellow and half of it blue, piercing it with a pencil, and spinning it. The colour you see while it is spinning is green.

FOLLOW-UP 3

An experiment which helps the children to experience the potential variety of mixed colours is as follows: Draw a series of rectangles, for example, six. Put yellow in the first one and blue in the last one. Now roughly grade the amount of each colour you put in the mixture, so that you have 90% yellow and 10% blue in square 2; 80% yellow and 20% blue in square 3, etc.

Do another parallel row of rectangles, this time using the same yellow but a different blue, and see how different the resulting greens are.

It is better to do this experiment with paints than with pens, because whatever you do, pens tend to give you the full strength of each colour!

FOLLOW-UP 4

Here are a few ideas for some freer mixing activities which the children will enjoy after the controlled experiments above:

1 Let them dampen the paper first and then watch the wet paints run into each other and create new colours, perhaps in the form of an arch like a rainbow.

2 Suggest they try mixing different greens to make a jungle picture.

3 Let them paint a picture of coloured spaghetti, or of coloured sweets in a space ship.

4 Ask the children to paint the colour of, for example: anger, joy, fun, happiness, fear, silence, cats, dogs. Let the children do it individually, then display their work and encourage them to compare their ideas. There can't be a right or wrong!

5 Show them this complementary colours experiment: use paint or colour on a simple drawing of a red car (about 4 cm in

length). Look at the red car for 30 seconds, then look at the paper next to it. *What can you see? I can see a green car.*

COMMENTS

1 Children often produce 'mud' because they don't clean their brushes out before selecting another colour, and then finish by mixing red, blue, and yellow. It is worth explaining this to them, and insisting on the professionalism of cleaning out the brush, swishing it to and fro in the water, and pouring out the bulk of the water inside the water jar.

2 A rather orangey-yellow mixed with a blue might produce a rather dull and dark green or even brown. The reason for this is that the colour you are calling yellow has red in it, and once you mix it with blue you have all three primaries together, and thus—brown!

For experiments in colour mixing, it is advisable to have:

A blue which is very slightly purpley, for example, ultramarine;
A slightly greeny blue, for example, prussian blue or cobalt;
A lemony yellow, for example, lemon yellow;
A warm yellow, for example, cadmium yellow;
A warm red, for example, crimson red;
A cool red, for example, vermillion.

3 The complement of a primary colour is made by mixing the other two primaries. So you could develop the following ideas and language:

Which is your favourite colour?
Which colours look nice together?
Green is the complement of red.
Purple is the complement of yellow.
Orange is the complement of blue.
People who have red hair often choose to wear green clothes.
People with more orangey hair often choose to wear blue clothes.

In other words, complementary colours enhance each other: they look good together!

This principle applies in colour combinations which are not clearly primary or secondary colours. For example, a mauvey grey might look beautiful with a yellowy brown.

The children do not need to know the 'grammar' of colour any more than they need to know the grammar of language. But growing familiarity with the effect of one colour on another can make a major contribution to a child's development: we are surrounded by colour!

4 If you have access to a good magnifying glass, you can show the children that colour photographs in books are made of tiny red, blue, yellow, and black dots. Thus green, for instance, is made of tiny dots of blue and yellow. Even better is to take the children to a local printing house, and ask the printer to show the basic colours that he/she uses.

6.2 Little black monster

The children draw and look at a little black monster. Then they look at a black piece of paper—and see a little white monster! They then draw more monsters and objects of their own, to repeat the same experiment.

In visual perception, this phenomena is known as persistence of vision.

LEVEL	Elementary
AGE	4–12
AIMS	**Language:** vocabulary enrichment; use of *can*. **Other:** to learn about the phenomenon of persistence of vision.
TIME	30 minutes
MATERIALS	For each child: a piece of white paper, a piece of black paper and a black felt-tip pen, and a sheet of paper with an outline of a little black monster on it.
PREPARATION	Draw a little black monster on a sheet of paper, or photocopy the one in the illustration.
IN CLASS	1 Show your copy of the little black monster.

Teacher: *What's this?*
Child: *A monster.*
Teacher: *What colour is it?*
Child: *It's black.*
Teacher: *Yes, it's a little black monster!*

Repeat this several times with several children.

2 Teacher: *But it is a very clever little monster! Sometimes it is black and sometimes it is white!*

Now give each child a copy of the outline of the little black monster. Ask them to fill it in with their black felt-tip pen.

3 Give each child a piece of black paper.

4 Ask the children to look at their little black monster for 20 seconds. The class count together.

Teacher: *Now look at the black paper. Don't stop! Look! Wait for the little monster! Can you see the little monster? Can you see a little white monster?*

5 The children can now draw other shapes, and ask their friends to try to see them in white on black paper.

6 Display the black drawings with the question pattern:

What can you see?
Can you see the little white …?

6.3 Coloured bird

Identifying and naming colours is followed by finding the colours in magazine pictures, cutting them out, and making a mosaic bird. This activity is best done with a small class.

LEVEL

Elementary

AGE

5–12

AIMS

Language: to practise the names of colours, and the vocabulary needed to describe a bird, and for talking about position.
Other: to learn how to make a mosaic.

TIME

30 minutes to collect enough squares of colour
30 minutes to make the picture

MATERIALS

An A2 or A1 sheet of white paper, glue sticks, several pairs of scissors; a large pile of old magazines, publicity material, etc. containing colourful pictures and photographs of mosaics (a mosaic is a picture or design made of small square pieces of stone, ceramic, or glass. Some of the most famous and beautiful examples are to be found in Ravenna, Italy); a 1 cm square of coloured paper for each pair of children (as an example of the size they must cut out).

PREPARATION

1 Draw on the paper a copy of the bird on Worksheet 6.3, page 154. Add the words as shown.

2 If you want to make it much easier for the children, cut strips of coloured paper 1.5 cm wide from magazine pictures, wrapping paper, or plain coloured paper. Then children only

have to snip off squares as they need them. Rather than scissors, the fastest way for you to cut long strips is to use a craft knife.

3 Make two paper stands for each group to store their coloured squares. Each stand is made of one piece of A4 paper, as shown in the illustration.

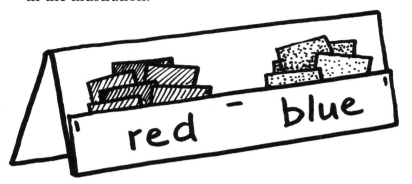

IN CLASS

1 Play an 'I-Spy' game with colour.

Teacher: *I can see/I spy something red.*
Child: *Is it the book?*
Teacher: *Yes!*

Revise and/or teach the words for colours: *red, blue, yellow, purple, orange, green, black, white.*

Let the children take over your role of 'spying'.

2 Change to another colour-practising game: Touch something red. The children have to stand up and do what you say.

3 Display the large picture of the bird.

Teacher: *Let's colour this bird! What does this say? Dark blue!*
Show me some dark blue in the room. So we must put dark blue at the top of the picture.

Explain that the children are going to find the colours in magazine pictures, cut them out in the form of small squares (about 1.5 cm), and then glue them into the right place on the large picture.

Suggest that the children collect lots of colours in the magazines before they decide what colour to make the bird itself. Say that it must be a magical bird!

4 Let the children work in groups to prepare their coloured squares, using the squares you have prepared for them as a guide to size. Some children can cut, and others can file into the paper stand (see above). While the children are happily cutting the squares, this is a good time for you to circulate and practise the language of colours:

Teacher: *What colours have you got?*
Child: *Red and green and ...*
Teacher: *That's a lovely colour! Which is your favourite colour?*
Which is a good colour for the bird/trees/sky? etc.

Notes
- The squares do not need to be absolutely identical in size but should be pretty near.
- The colours in any one area do not need to be identical: some variety is an advantage.
- An alternative to gluing the whole back of the paper is to glue just the top part, and so create an effect of feathers. In this case, the children will have to start gluing the colours from the bottom, after which it is easy to overlap them slightly.

5 After a few minutes, stop the children and ask what colours they have got:

Teacher: *What colours have you got? Have you got blue? Is it dark blue or light blue?*

Show examples to demonstrate the meaning of *dark* and *light*.

Begin to decide with the children which colours they want to make the bird. Each part of its body should be different (beak, head, body, wing, tail, legs). Write the colours onto each part.

6 Appoint two judges. When the children have got about 10 squares ready they will have to go to the judges, decide what the colour is, and then decide where to stick it. You can keep a supervisory role.

Child judge: *What colour is it?*
Child: *Blue.*
Child judge: *Is it dark blue or light blue?*
Child: *It's dark blue.*
Child judge: *Yes, you are right. Stick it on the sky, at the top.*

Every so often, give other children the role of judge.

7 As the children complete the bird, point out to them how lovely colour looks when it has variety in it (the slight changes of colour within one general colour).

FOLLOW-UP

Once the bird is made it can't be just left! It is a magical bird! It needs a name, a place to live, and adventures to have.

6.4 Matching colours

The children work on their ability to judge the colour of an object, and then begin to match this colour with their crayons.

LEVEL

Elementary and upwards

AGE

8–12

AIMS

Language: to practise the vocabulary of colours and shades of colour.

Other: to realize that each object has its own special colour or variety of colours, and to try to match them.

TIME

30 minutes

MATERIALS

For each child: Coloured pencils (rather than pens) in a fair range of colours and several small pieces of plain white paper.

IN CLASS

1 Ask what the colour is of various objects in the class, for example, the board, the wall, your desk, a book.

2 Describe the colour of something, and ask what the children think it is.

Teacher: *It's yellow.*
Child: *Is it the book?*
Teacher: *No.*
Child: *Is it your desk?*
Teacher: *Yes.*

During the conversation, make the point that each colour is special.

3 Now place a piece of white paper where all the children can see it—on the board, for example. Say that you are going to try to make it the same colour as the wall. Start off by colouring it lightly, then gradually make the colour darker until it is the same. Talk as you try to match the colour, for example:

It's yellow. It's a light yellow.

4 Take the piece of paper you have coloured and hold it against the wall. Ask questions like these:

Teacher: *Is it the same colour? Is it too dark or too light? Is it too yellow?*
Child: *It's too light!*
Teacher: *Can you make it darker?*
Child: *Yes!*

5 The children now work in pairs and try to colour at least two pieces of paper so that they match an object in the room. You take part in their work, making use of the language of the activity.

6 Pairs then exchange papers and try to identify what each patch of colour represents:

Child: *What's this?*
Child: *It's the wall.*
Child: *Is it right?*
Child: *Yes, it is./No, it isn't. It's too dark/light.*

7 Exhibit all the pieces of paper and caption them, for example,

The wall is light yellow. Andrew and John.

FOLLOW-UP

Either ask the children to work outside, or to bring in objects and materials from outside, for example:

bark from a tree
leaves
a painted piece of wood
a mat
a piece of cloth
a coat

The children try to reproduce the colours of these items on paper with their coloured pencils.

7 Design

In this book, design is interpreted to mean making visual images for a particular communicative purpose, rather than for personal expression.

The principles of design given in this section are relevant to all types of publication, from books to websites to posters for lost dogs.

It is important to make a collection and display of examples of graphic design from the children's world, and to help them to begin to learn the language of design, which will affect them so much in their everyday lives.

Graphic design, as a language, is as varied as the communicative intentions of the designers, which may include any of the following:

- to engage and interest
- to be clear
- to show the viewer which is the important part of the message
- to communicate the order in which the elements of the message should be read
- to communicate seriousness, frivolity, fun, excitement, sensuality, tradition, fashion, etc.

There is no reason why the young child should not begin to appreciate some of these intentions, just as he or she might begin to appreciate them in music or in texts. However, as a general approach, we suggest that you concentrate on helping the child to achieve the following:

- showing what is the most important part of a design, for example, the title of a book
- enjoying the shapes, colours, tones, and other qualities of the medium they are using
- learning how to make a message effective by thinking about what they want to communicate, to whom, and in what kind of situation.

These are the principle elements in design, and there is no reason for not beginning to raise awareness of them early in a child's life.

7.1 Advertisements

In this activity the children collect as many advertisements as they can find, including English texts, and make an evaluation of their appeal.

LEVEL

Lower-intermediate and above

AGE

8–12

AIMS

Language: to practise language for giving opinions and reasons.
Other: to make a poster; to gain confidence in expressing likes and dislikes, and justifying them.

TIME

45 minutes for discussing the designs, carrying out the survey, and categorizing the designs
45 minutes (or more if possible) for designing and making a poster

MATERIALS

A collection of advertisements; paper, pencils, glue.

PREPARATION

About a week before the lesson, ask the children to collect advertisements and bring them to class. Show them examples of advertisements aimed at three categories of people: children, teenagers, and adults. As the examples arrive, get the children to put them in different piles. Ask:

Teacher: *Is this for children, teenagers, or adults?*
Child: *It's for adults.*
Teacher: *OK, put it on that table, please.*

IN CLASS

1 Ask each of the children to look at the examples and (if there are enough) to choose one from each category. Have a general discussion to introduce the ideas and the language of the activity:

Do you like this design: very much/a little bit/not very much?
I like it/don't like it/quite like it.
It's serious/etc.
The colour/picture/letters look/s nice/funny/old-fashioned/modern beautiful/ugly/boring/interesting/exciting.
This is the most exciting/etc.

2 Each pair of children now selects one example from the six they have chosen, show it to at least five other pairs of children, and ask them to say whether they like it very much, not very much, or not at all. Their findings should be entered into their survey sheet.

Child A: *Do you like it very much, or not very much, or not at all?*
Child B: *I like it very much./I don't like it very much./I don't like it at all.*

> ## Designer's Survey
> Choose one of these sentences:
> I like it very much.
> I don't like it very much.
> I don't like it at all.

3 At the end of the survey, the results should be added up, and each design categorized and displayed as being very good/not very good/poor.

4 Discuss with the children some of the factors which make a design successful. Of course, children are not sophisticated enough, and do not have enough language, to explore such matters in depth, but introducing the idea that designs can be evaluated is already a step forward.

If the children don't think of these points, introduce them yourself in the mother tongue:

The main lettering must be big and clear.
The picture must have a strong shape, and be relevant to the message of the poster.
The words must be relevant to the message, and as few as possible.
People must know what they have to do, for example, who they must contact to say that they have a dog for sale.

5 The children now design a poster of their own. They might like to choose from the following list, or design a poster to meet a particular need of their own at the moment:

Poster design for:

a lost cat
a dog they would like to have
a party
a new bar of chocolate
a litter campaign.

The criteria for a good design might be:

Can you see it (from ten metres)?
Can you understand it (the idea, and what it is trying to say)?
Do you like it? (Is it beautiful and/or interesting and/or a good idea?)

7.2 Birthday card

The principles of design given in this activity relate directly to book covers, book pages, posters, and greetings cards, all of which children can make.

LEVEL

Elementary and above

AGE

5–12

AIMS

Language: to learn/practise language for expressing opinions and giving reasons; the language of greetings.
Other: to make a card; graphic design; to gain confidence in expressing likes and dislikes.

TIME

40 minutes to collect, display, and evaluate examples of graphic design

60 minutes for the children to design and make a birthday card

MATERIALS

A collection of examples of graphic design, particularly birthday cards, a guillotine (paper cutter).

For each child: a piece of thin, white A4 card and (if you want the children to post their cards to real people) an A5 envelope, pens and pencils.

PREPARATION

1 A few days before the lesson, ask the children to look at home for old birthday cards, and bring them into the lesson.

2 To give variety, you might like to use the school guillotine (a paper-cutter) to cut different sizes of paper (but do not let young children use it unsupervised).

IN CLASS

1 Look at the examples of cards you have collected. Show each one, and get the class to vote on whether it is attractive or not. According to the language level and sophistication of the children, begin to introduce the sort of language they can use to say why they like or don't like the design. You can make a separate display of all the designs which nobody likes. Create an atmosphere of respect for minority views.

  While your aim is to focus the children's minds on what makes a good design, in the end, it must remain subjective.

2 Introduce the idea of designing a birthday card for a particular person. The children can choose someone known to them, for example, a member of their family, or one of their other classmates, or someone else, such as the school caretaker. If they have already invented one they could choose a manikin character (see 2.4).

3 Have a class brainstorming discussion to establish the following:

– which words are needed. The minimum must be *Happy Birthday!* Other texts might include *I wish you a Happy Birthday! A Happy Birthday from Tom to Grandad!*
– what picture he or she might like.
– whether to put the picture in a rectangle, a circle, or an irregular shape or to let the picture go off the sides. Draw these choices on the board:

rectangle   irregular   off both sides   circle

4 Show the class the simplest fold, which is to fold the card from A4 to A5. You might like to show additional folds.

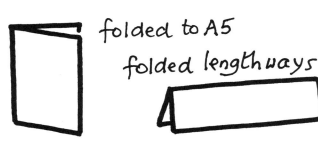

folded to A5
folded lengthways

zigzag

folded diagonally

5 The children design their cards, display them, and finally send them to the lucky birthday boy, girl, or grown-up!

COMMENTS

1 Because the lettering is important within the design, it might be helpful if the children do a lettering activity first (see 7.4, 'Designing your name').

2 As a general guiding principle, the criteria for what is good should not rest on the neatness and regularity of the lettering and lines used, but on the strength of the main message, and on the richness of the shapes, colours, etc.

FOLLOW-UP

The children can also design and make other cards for other festivals such as Christmas, New Year, Diwali, Eid, St Valentine's Day, Mother's Day, Father's Day, as well as sending congratulations and 'Get Well' greetings.

7.3 Coat of arms

A 'coat of arms' is a picture symbol representing an individual, a family, or an institution. Originally, the reason for having a 'coat of arms' ('arms' as in 'weapons') was to identify knights dressed from top to toe in armour. However, 'coats of arms' have come to be used for a much wider range of purposes since those days, with the logos of modern companies an obvious example.

Designing a coat of arms requires consideration of (a) what ideas best represent the individual, company, etc., and (b) the form of the picture symbols. In this activity the children design a coat of arms for themselves, and if there is time, perhaps another one for the school.

LEVEL	**Elementary and upwards**
AGE	**4–12** The symbolic considerations behind a coat of arms will be difficult for young children to grasp, and you may just get individual pictures. Nevertheless, it is worth doing, even with the very young.
AIMS	**Language:** vocabulary extension. It is difficult to predict what the children will ask for. Have a dictionary ready! **Other:** to appreciate the use of symbols to represent values, characteristics, etc.
TIME	**60 minutes**
MATERIALS	A photocopy of Worksheet 7.3, page 155.
PREPARATION	For each child: an A4 sheet of plain paper, an A5 piece of card, enough self-adhesive clear plastic to cover the A5 card, and coloured pens.
IN CLASS	1 Show the children examples of coats of arms. 2 Match words and phrases that explain some of the coats of arms. 3 Ask the children to brainstorm ideas for what they might include on a coat of arms for their class or school. This will show them how to look for original ideas, and ways of representing them. Here are some of the ideas which might be taken up for a school coat of arms:

- *several children*
- *books*
- *computers*
- *nature*
- *games*
- *help, shown with holding hands*
- *happiness, shown with a smiling mouth*
- *ideas, shown with a light bulb*
- *growing up, shown with two trees, one big and one small*

4 The children do their design on A5 paper with a thick pen.

5 If you want the children to write, help them to find a short phrase to add to their design. For example:

- *Love and learning*
- *Happiness*
- *Children and teachers*

Note: This step will only be possible with older children. Most young children will not naturally think in abstract terms.

6 Use the photocopying machine to reduce the children's designs to a small size—about 5 cm, for example. Stick them onto cards to make badges. After they've coloured their badges, you can cover them with self-adhesive clear plastic.

7 Display the badges in the classroom or, if possible, in the school reception area.

FOLLOW-UP

Expand the study of 'coats of arms' into the many company logos which the children see every day.

7.4 Designing your name

Some teachers are happy for the children to make use of writing in their early years of English. This activity is for them. Designing letters is a wonderful way for the children to experience the essential characteristics of each letter they work on.

It is difficult for children and, indeed, for untrained adults, to create good title lettering. The most common fault is to think that properly typeset letters must be imitated by hand, which is almost impossible.

In handmade lettering, the most important thing is to avoid detailed regularity! Make the letters characterful. The easiest letters to do are ones that are very fat and close together—this gives them great strength. An alternative is to make the letters very thin!

In this activity the children try to invent at least three different ways of writing their name. See Worksheet 7.4, page 156, which offers examples of letters the children might like to use. Collect other examples which you think the children could do versions of.

LEVEL	**All**
AGE	**5–12**

AIMS

Language: to learn the language of praise and guidance used by you; to be able to say the alphabet in English.
Other: hand–eye co-ordination; to appreciate the varied designs of letters.

TIME

40 minutes to design different versions of the letter 'A'
40 minutes to design one or two name-strip cards

MATERIALS

Strips of white paper or card for each child. These should be at least 5 cm by 20 cm (you might find what you want for free amongst the waste paper thrown away by a local printer); a copy of Worksheet 7.4, page 156, showing the examples of lettering; glue; scissors.

PREPARATION

1 To make sure you feel confident that you can do different letters reasonably well, do one or two versions of your own name (or that of a child or pet).
2 Draw an 'A' in outline on a very large sheet of coloured paper, and cut it out. The children draw more As, and stick them inside your big letter A.
3 Make a collection of different letter designs—preferably large letters, and drawn by hand.

IN CLASS

1 The aim of the first and second steps is to help the children to play with the shapes of letters, and to realize that there are many ways of representing each letter.

Begin by drawing the letter A on the board, and asking the children to identify it. Let the children see you do more designs for A (don't prepare them—the action is important). Show them the big cut-out A you have prepared. Say that you want them to make lots of letter As and to stick them onto the big A.

2 Give the children several small pieces of paper to design their As on. Encourage them to experiment. You could also give them coloured paper, scrap materials (cloth, cotton wool, sticks), and invite the children to make letters to glue on to the large A.

3 The next objective is to extend this experiment by getting the children to design letters for their names. Give each child a strip of paper or card. If you think it will be helpful for them, give each pair of children a copy of the sample letters on Worksheet 7.4. Ask the children to design at least two different versions of their name.

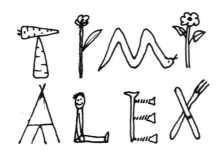
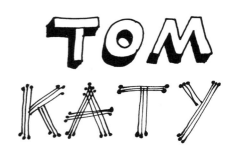

FOLLOW-UP 1 Help the children to experiment with different ways of making letters, using huge letters on paper and card, three-dimensional letters made out of polystyrene foam or branches, etc., and a mime performed with their own bodies.

FOLLOW-UP 2 Whenever appropriate, take the opportunity to show the children examples of letter design in publicity material, etc., by printing out different letter designs offered on your computer.

7.5 Picture picnics

Mind maps or idea webs have become a well-known resource, and are useful in art and design education, as well as in language learning.

The spreading design of *webs* helps the brain to spread its rich resources, whereas *lists* of ideas tend to keep the brain on a logical road of known ideas. Idea webs are thus perfect for developing creativity and fresh ideas. And creativity is the basis of art.

Idea webs are also relevant in second language acquisition because they lead to associations of ideas which would not otherwise take place. The ideas can be noted down in the mother tongue or in English in the web. Once the brainstorming of the web is over, some words can be translated from mother tongue to English if necessary. In this activity the ideas are represented by pictures.

I have used the term 'picture picnic' because children like to be able to identify an activity with a familiar and pleasurable association—not too abstract like the conventional 'mind map', or possibly unpleasant like a 'spider's web'. 'Picnic' because you collect together lots of things to eat and then you dip into the different ideas wherever you like—without following a fixed progression as you would in a formal dinner!

LEVEL **Beginners and above**

AGE 5–12

AIMS **Language:** spoken vocabulary practice on a theme.
Other: to express ideas and links between them graphically; to encourage creativity.

TIME	**40 minutes**
MATERIALS	A large piece of paper, for example, A2; broad coloured pens; an A3 sheet of white paper for each child.
IN CLASS	1 Begin by demonstrating the concept of 'idea webbing' or 'idea picnics'. Ask a child to draw a simple picture symbol in the middle of the paper representing their school. Allow 30 seconds for this. Ten seconds may be enough!
	2 Ask other children to call out what they associate with school, and then to come and draw a very simple picture symbol of their board. It should either be directly related to the picture of the school or related through another picture already drawn.

3 Look for opportunities to make one idea come out of another, then join the two with a line or with a picture. Talk about the ideas and how they are linked.

If you have done any of the other activities on the use of picture symbols you can use the same symbols again (see 7.6 and 7.7). You can decide whether to allow some written words, or to insist on the use of picture symbols only.

FOLLOW-UP

Other subjects for idea picnics which can be displayed and talked about afterwards:

- a friend: things they have at home, things they can and can't do, things they like and don't like, friends and family, places they go to, their day, hobbies
- my day (for present simple descriptions)
- what I did yesterday (for past tense descriptions)
- what I will do tomorrow or in the future generally (for future tense descriptions)
- a story I have read/heard
- a song I have learnt
- time (an example of how idea picnics can be used in discussions to explore an area full of objective and subjective associations, and which demand a higher level of proficiency in the language)
- one of my problems, and possible answers to it (an example of the way that idea picnics can be used at a higher level).

COMMENTS

Help the children to appreciate the idea that webs can be coloured for decorative, symbolic, or diagrammatic reasons. Also show them how graphic symbols can be used, including pictures, of course, but also circles, squares, thick and thin lines, etc.

7.6 Picture symbols in a town

The children study picture symbols representing the activities people can do in Whitby, a little seaside holiday town in North Yorkshire, England. They go on to design picture symbols for their own town or district.

In the follow-up, they can broaden their study to include picture symbols used in other areas of daily life, for example, computer icons, traffic signs, video players, and packaging design.

Picture symbols are being used increasingly, and children can be encouraged from an early age to become 'picture-symbol literate'. As well as learning the meaning of existing ones, they can also develop critical awareness by designing their own symbols.

LEVEL

Elementary and upwards

AGE

4–12 (although only older children will be able to think of designs which are universal, rather than individual examples)

AIMS

Language: the present continuous of verbs of activity; *can*, as in *You can swim there.* The picture symbols you add to the activity will determine the language practised.
Other: to design picture symbols.

TIME

30–40 minutes on the study of existing picture symbols
60 minutes for the development, design, and testing of their own picture symbols

MATERIALS

A copy of Worksheet 7.6, page 157, for each pair of children.

PREPARATION

1 Collect as many different picture symbols as you can from magazines, instruction manuals, etc.

   Prepare basic questions and answers related to the symbols:

   Teacher: *What does this picture mean?*
   Child: *It means 'You can play tennis here.'*
   Child: *It means 'There is a restaurant.'*

2 Find out if picture symbols are used in the school in places you could take the class to see. Prepare basic questions and answers related to the symbols:

   Teacher: *What does this picture mean?*
   Child: *It means 'This is dangerous.'*

3 Check that the language required to talk about the symbols is language known to the children. Decide which language must be revised or introduced.

IN CLASS

1 Draw on the board one of the picture symbols from Worksheet 7.6 (choose one that is relevant to your children).

Teacher: *What's he doing?*
Child: *He's swimming.*
Teacher: *That's right. He's swimming. People can swim in Whitby. Here's Whitby* (holding up the Worksheet to show the little town on the map).

2 Draw another of the picture symbols.

Teacher: *What's she doing?*
Child: *She's playing tennis.*
Teacher: *That's right. You can play tennis in Whitby, and you can swim in Whitby. It's a nice place!*
Can you swim/play tennis in (home town or district)?

3 Continue with some of the other symbols. Change the questions.

Teacher: *Can you sail in Whitby?*
Child: *Yes, you can.*

4 Now look at the symbols, and talk about the other things that can be done in Whitby.

5 Ask the children, in pairs, to draw similar picture symbols to show what can be done in their home town or district. Picture symbols do not usually rely on detail *within* the overall shape, but on the shape itself. The children usually try to draw a picture full of details instead of concentrating on the overall shape. It might, therefore, be better to ask the children to cut their picture symbol out of coloured paper before sticking it into a rectangle of a different, contrasting colour (or black and white, if you haven't got colours).

I suggest displaying the children's picture symbols on one large chart with a heading such as 'What we can do in our town!'

VARIATION

The children test each of their picture symbols on at least eight other children, and each picture will only be accepted if at least five children interpret it as intended. The children should make up the tests, orally or in writing, for their own pictures. The questions should be multiple choice, with three possible answers.

FOLLOW-UP 1

Picture symbols play such a major role in our lives, and relate to so many everyday topics, that they lend themselves to further study. Here are some more examples you might like to follow up:

Road safety
children crossing
zebra crossing
steep hill
bends
ice
wind
deer
main road
stop
slow
road repairs

Concepts
right … this is right
wrong … this is wrong
good idea … this is a good idea
like/love … I love New York

Instructions
Be careful!
Recycle

Put your litter in the bin.
Go this way.
You must not smoke here.
You must not swim here.
You must not camp here.
Dogs must not come here.

CD players
Stop
Play
Loud
Quiet
Rewind
Fast forward
Eject

Information
Telephone … there is a
telephone here
Toilets … there is a toilet here
first aid … there is first aid here

Weather
Cloudy … it was/will be cloudy
Rainy … it was/will be rainy
sunny …

Money
Pounds
Dollars

Maps
mountains
hills
road
motorway
path
river
lake
forest
house
church
castle
bridge

FOLLOW-UP 2

Take the children to see and interpret picture symbols used in the school and/or show them others you have collected, and ask them to say what they mean.

You can do this as a survey, in which you brainstorm with the children at least three interpretations for each picture and write them on the board. Ask each child to decide which interpretation he or she thinks is intended, and then decide which pictures are the most successful by being the least ambiguous.

If the idea of making picture symbols merely involves copying those given here, you might like to extend the activity by asking the children to design symbols for each facility in the school: classroom, store room, teachers' room, toilet, gymnasium, etc.

FOLLOW-UP 3

Road signs are of particular relevance to children, and they could usefully make copies of all the road signs near their school. Note the use of:

- triangles for warning
- circles for imperatives
- rectangles for information

7.7 Picture symbols for language practice

The children are challenged to design and draw a variety of picture symbols to represent the language they know and the patterns you want them to practise.

LEVEL

Beginners and upwards

AGE

4–12

AIMS

Language: Vocabulary and patterns you want the children to practise. In this example we have used food vocabulary and *love* and *like*.
Other: to draw picture symbols; to practise using the visual memory.

TIME

30 minutes minimum

MATERIALS

Pictures of food and drink (or whatever nouns you want to practise) either from magazines and/or from your own drawings.

PREPARATION

Cut suitable pictures out of magazines, etc., or draw them.

IN CLASS

1 Show the picture of ice cream:

Teacher: *I like ice-cream! Do you like ice-cream?*
Child A: *Yes.*
Child B: *Yes.*
etc.
Teacher: *Yes, we like ice-cream!*

2 Draw an ice-cream (or ask a child to draw it for you) on the right hand side of the board.

Teacher: *What does this mean?*
Child: *Ice-cream.*

Draw a heart to the left of the ice-cream.

Teacher: *What does this mean?*
Child: *Like.*

Draw a person to the left of the heart with one arm pointing onto his own chest.

Teacher: *What does this mean?*
Child: *I*

3 Now repeat the drawings but this time draw two figures to represent 'we'.

4 Ask the children to draw these two lines of drawings in their books, and to add the sentences: *I like ice-cream. We like ice-cream.*

5 Ask the children to take at least one other popular food, draw the three pictures for *I* and *we*, and write the sentence. Example: *I like cake. We like cake.*

6 Now choose a food which some of the children will not like, or even make a joke, and show a picture of an old sock or old boot!

7 Ask the children to write and illustrate three more sentences about food and drink that they don't like.

8 You can extend the activity by introducing more subject pronouns (such as *we*), by introducing 'love' as a heart with ticks added, or by adding more hearts!

VARIATION

Similar lessons can be based on the same idea of creating pictures to illustrate sentence patterns. Here are some examples:

Example 1
like plus *-ing*

You   like   swimming.

Example 2
have

I   have got   a dog.

Example 3
am plus feelings

I am   angry.

Example 4
can/can't

I   can   ride a bike.

Example 5
favourite

Alex's   favourite   drink is apple juice.

FOLLOW-UP 1

The children can try to illustrate every word they know as a class, and to make a large wall chart of their agreed pictures. It would be interesting for the children to discover that they have to find abstract symbols for some words ('like' symbolized by a heart, 'right' and 'wrong' symbolized by a tick and a cross), and that others must just remain as words, because no-one could find any suitable abstract symbols!

If you and the children like this approach, it could become a regular technique for you to use.

FOLLOW-UP 2

You might judge that the children are sophisticated enough to be interested in the history of writing, which began as pictures and picture symbols, and that they might like to carry out their own experiment, related to the way pictures can change from naturalism, through simple pictographs, to abstract shapes.

1 Put the children into a circle, or organize a sequenced route, so that they can all pass the picture they are going to work with in the same direction— passing on to the person to their right, and receiving from the person to their left.

2 Give each child an A4 piece of paper, torn in half vertically. Show the children how to fold the paper in half once, twice, and then again, so that it is divided by the marks of the folds into eight sections.

3 Each child should then draw a simple picture in the top section. Give them exactly one minute to do this. Explain that they will be passing their papers to their right, and that their partner will have exactly ten seconds to look at the picture before folding it over. Their neighbour must then draw in the second panel what he or she remembers of the drawing. The papers are passed along between seven children before being returned to their originator, opened out, and exhibited. In order to demonstrate the principle of the activity—which is that we always simplify what we see to make it recognizable to us and memorable—if all goes well, as the drawings are copied and re-copied they will become more and more simplified. This makes the point about the change from pictures, which were used until about 3000 BC, to cuneiform writing after that date.

Conclude by showing the children examples of the changes to writing which took place over thousands of years, and compare that experience with the way their own pictures changed over a period of just a few minutes!

Evolution of Japanese Kanji

tree

Sun

Acknowledgements
I am grateful to William Chuckney, who heightened my awareness of the potential of pictographs in language learning.

7.8 Pop-up cards

Children love making pop-ups, and they are surprisingly easy to make! They are particularly effective for exhibitions. The only disadvantage of them is that you cannot make copies! So, who finally keeps them?

As a guiding principle, it is better to make the pop-up design first, and then decide what you want to write and draw on it.

In this activity we are going to describe how to make a very simple greeting card with a single pop-up.

LEVEL	**All**
AGE	7–12
AIMS	**Language:** your language of guidance and encouragement in the making of the pop-ups; the greetings written in the cards. **Other:** to learn how to make a pop-up card.

TIME	**40 minutes for a single pop-up greeting card with one picture and one line of text**
MATERIALS	For each child: an A4 sheet of thin white card (or paper, if card isn't available), some smaller pieces of card and paper, pencils, coloured pens, scissors.
PREPARATION	1 Prepare beforehand: a) the A5 folded card with one corner folded over, and b) the same but with a bunch of paper flowers glued into position (see the illustration below). 2 For the very young ones, fold all the cards from A4 to A5, then fold down the upper corner. Open each card, then press the fold downwards inside the fold of the card before shutting it (see illustration).
IN CLASS	1 Give each child a piece of A4 card, and demonstrate how to fold it.

Fold the corner back, then inwards.
Fold A4 to A5

open and the fold lifts.

Glue flowers to the fold.

2 Let the children open and close the card, and watch how the fold stands up as they open it.

3 Show your example of paper flowers stuck onto the fold and lifting up as you open the card.

Discuss what other things could 'come out' of the card. Help the children to feel that anything is possible. (Examples: flowers, child with raised arms and happy smile, bird, monster, dog, rocket.)

4 Give out the bits of card. Show how whatever they draw and cut out must be folded in the middle before being glued to the fold.

VARIATION	The children can make complete books out of different kinds of pop-ups. Having made the book, the children make pictures out of the pop-ups, then write a story to go with what they have made. See *Creating Stories with Children* in this series.

7.9 Postcards

There is a wonderful sense of purpose for a child in designing and sending a postcard to someone they know. The writing is not just marked by you and left in an exercise book!

LEVEL   **Elementary and above**

AGE   **6–12 (or from the age at which writing is introduced)**

AIMS   **Language:** fluency in writing.
                   Other: to make and send a personal message with a meaningful picture as well as words; graphic design.

TIME   **30–40 minutes**

MATERIALS   For each child: several pieces of thin white card about 15 cm x 11 cm.

PREPARATION   Try to find postcards or greeting cards which show both pictures as well as text, to give the children an idea of what you have in mind.

IN CLASS   1 Show the children cards you have collected and tell them you would like them to design, write, and illustrate some similar cards to send to people they know.

2 Let the children have a blank card immediately rather than ask them to plan their story and picture on paper beforehand. It is important for them to feel the card and its size, and to imagine it arriving by post. This will help them to decide what they want to do.

If the children make a mistake, it is better to give them another piece of card rather than ask them to do a sketch first, and then lose their creative drive later on, when they add the final design to the card.

Discuss with the children what they might do. Here are some examples:

– Draw a picture of your room and write about the things in it you like best; for example, My favourite toy is my teddy bear. My favourite book is *Winnie the Pooh.* My favourite CD is *Witches,* by the Raves.

– Draw a picture from your imagination of the person you are writing to and what you think they might be doing at that moment and write about it, for example, At this moment, I think you are cooking. You are boiling the vegetables. And you are reading a book!

– Draw a picture from imagination of the person you are writing to doing something really amazing, and perhaps crazy and funny, too, and write about it. For example, You are flying. You have wings. There is a big bird! It is coming!

– Draw a picture from imagination of the person you are writing to which shows your favourite memory of being with them. Write about it. For example, Last Christmas! It was wonderful! You were very funny! You wore a Father Christmas beard but you wore Dracula teeth. I laughed!

– Draw a picture and write a story about it—perhaps about an amazing animal you found and looked after. For example, I found a little dragon in the garden. It was hiding under a bush. I said, 'Hello little dragon! What's your name', and it said, 'Hello little dragon! What's your name?' And I said, 'Andrew!' And it said, 'Andrew!' And I said, 'What's your name?' And it said, 'What's your name?'

3 Discuss some basic ideas with the class. If you like, you might write the ideas on the board:

Side 1: *A picture and 10 to 20 words.*
Side 2: *A letter of 10 to 20 words.*

4 As the children work on their cards you can circulate (a) giving encouraging comments, (b) showing interest, (c) making suggestions. (See page 13 for useful language.)

5 Have an exhibition of the cards before they are sent. Discuss them. Ask the children to read out what they have written, and to talk about what they have done.

VARIATION 1 Make the most of any child sending their card to another town or country. Look it up on the map, etc. Also go to the post office with the children and get them to buy the stamps and post the cards.

VARIATION 2 Exhibit the cards in the school lobby or a local bank, etc.

COMMENTS This is an opportunity to introduce the children to the whole idea of design, rather than just drawing a picture. The shape of their picture must be characterful and striking in its relationship with the rectangular shape of the card. It is not just a matter of drawing something so that it is recognizable.

7.10   'You and them' books

Very young children get enormous satisfaction from illustrating a book based on a story they have made up. This will be one of their first experiences of the relationship between text and pictures. It is also something wonderful for them to take home!

LEVEL	Pre-intermediate
AGE	6–12
AIMS	**Language:** this depends on the story you make up or choose. **Other:** to illustrate a story and help make a book.
TIME	**20 minutes making up a story with the children** **40 minutes for the children's illustrations**
MATERIALS	An A3 sheet of paper, scissors and glue, a typewriter or word-processor (or neat writing!), pencils or crayons.

PREPARATION

1 Take the piece of A3 paper and fold it into a book measuring 21 x 15 cm, like this:

A3 folded to A5   nearly 15cm   text lines 11 cm

2 Measure what you consider would be a reasonable length of text line for you to type. In this book the lines are no more than 12 cm long, to make it easy to find the next line.

IN CLASS

1 Make up a story with the children, or choose a story they already know.

Later, out of class, type the text using a point size of between 14 and 18 cm, according to the length of the story. You need to make it fit onto the three text pages of the book, leaving room for a picture on each page. Type the title of the story in the largest letters that will fit on the cover, which is 15 cm wide. The most effective way to do this is to centre the title, the name of the class (or children), and the date. (Alternatively, you could create the front cover using design software.)

2 Print out the text. Divide it into three parts. Glue each part onto one of the three text pages. Glue the title onto the front title page.

3 Open out the paper so that it is A3 again, then make one photocopy for each child.

4 Show the book to the children in the next lesson. Tell them what the text is about on each page. Discuss which picture

should go on each page, relevant to the text on that page. Discuss which picture should go on the front.

5 The children do their pictures.

6 Photocopy the books so that the children can take copies home. Put one in the school library, etc.

COMMENTS

You can make books once the children can co-operate with you to make up a story in English. See *Creating Stories with Children* in this series.

7.11 Zig-zag books

The Zig-zag books in this activity are the easiest books to make, since they require no cutting or gluing and are made out of ordinary white paper.

The design gives 7 small pages (10 cm x 15 cm) plus the cover. If the children are going to write, this means putting just one sentence and one illustration on each page.

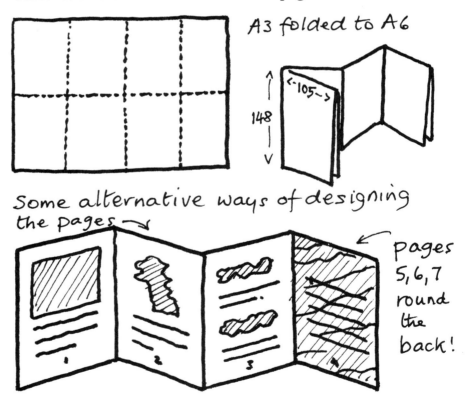

Because they are made out of one piece of A3 paper, the books cannot be expanded, so they can be used for texts which are fixed in length, but are not suitable for an on-going journal. But you can photocopy them, so you, the school library, and the children's family and neighbours, can all have a copy.

LEVEL	Elementary and above
AGE	6–12 (as soon as writing is acceptable and possible)
AIMS	**Language:** to write a personal profile, using the language of the first year of English. **Other:** to make a book.
TIME	**Approximately two hours**
MATERIALS	An A3 sheet of paper and coloured pencils or pens for each child.
PREPARATION	Prepare a sample book about yourself, or about a puppet or toy animal the children know.
IN CLASS	1 Show the children the book you have prepared.

2 Go through the topics you think they could have for each page.

  Here are some examples for the 7 pages of the book:
  - *This is me. I am (eight).*
  - *I have (two parents and one brother).*
  - *I have a pet. It is (a cat). Its name is (Bodil).*
  - *My favourite food is (fish fingers and chips).*
  - *I like (playing with my friends).*
  - *I don't like (cleaning).*
  - *I want (my own computer).*

3 Summarize on the board what the children have to do. Include the words for the front cover, and some sample sentences.

4 Give out the A3 sheets of paper. Show the children how to fold them (see the illustration).

The children should copy what you do, fold by fold!

A3 in half lengthways

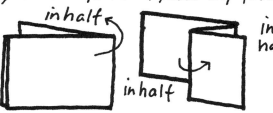

5 Guide and encourage the children as they make their books.

6 Display the books or photocopy them and distribute them to interested people.

VARIATION	You and the children might like to make a large class sized zig-zag book. Each child will need one or two pieces of A5 white paper, which will be stuck into the zig-zag book when they have been written and illustrated. For the zig zag book itself you must buy the biggest sheets of thin coloured card you can find and then cut them into strips which are at least 22 cm in height. Fold the strips into sections which are big enough to stick the A5 sheets on. You need one page for each child, so for a class book you must stick several strips together.

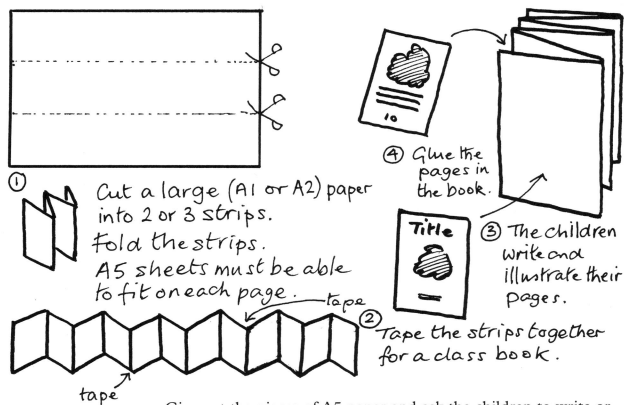

① Cut a large (A1 or A2) paper into 2 or 3 strips.
Fold the strips.
A5 sheets must be able to fit on each page.

tape

② Tape the strips together for a class book.

③ The children write and illustrate their pages.

④ Glue the pages in the book.

Title

tape

Give out the pieces of A5 paper and ask the children to write or draw their own page, according to the topic you have chosen. When their work is ready it can be glued into the zig-zag book.

Possible topics for a class zig-zag book might be:

– a picture dictionary
– a class 'strange creature' or monster
– a special display book by the children about their town and their school for international visitors, a tourist board in the town hall, etc.
– a tour guide book for an imaginary town created by children
– class year book
– a story book.

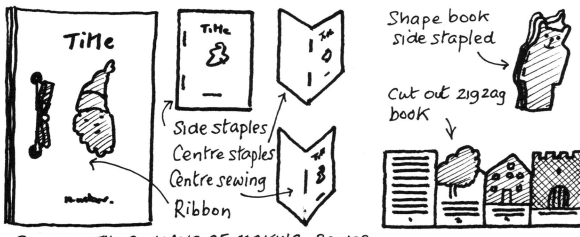

Title

Side staples
Centre staples
Centre sewing
Ribbon

Shape book side stapled

Cut out zigzag book

SOME OTHER WAYS OF MAKING BOOKS

8 Technology

Although the three activities given in this section are quite time-consuming, they are all immensely rich in their potential to motivate the interest of the children, to make them want to use English well, to help them to remember the English related to the activity and to help both them and the school to impress the parents!

8.1 The overhead projector

The overhead projector (OHP) is increasingly common in schools, but its potential for artistic expression and for language practice is little known. Of course, simple pictures can be drawn on transparencies, and projected, but a great variety of textures can be used in the picture-making, and projected in an effective way. Grass, plants, and flowers, for example, look very beautiful when projected! Let the children experiment!

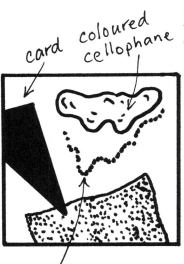

A story-show with an overhead-projector, combined with sound effects, can make a very impressive performance for parents at the end of term!

LEVEL	**All**
AGE	**4–12**
AIMS	**Language:** to improve fluency; questions and descriptions. **Other:** Experimenting with making shapes from unusual materials; imagination.
TIME	**40–60 minutes**

MATERIALS

Overhead projector and screen, paper, thin card, scissors, any objects and materials which might look interesting on the screen (wool, feathers, grass, leaves, torn paper, cloth, plastic, string), toy animals, and an OHP pen and a small piece of transparency (5 cm x 5 cm) for each child.

IN CLASS

1 Put a piece of card around the OHP screen so that the class cannot see what is being laid on it. Switch on the OHP, and place an object—a ruler, for example—on the screen. Ask the children what they think it is. Invite individual children to come to the OHP and put an object on the screen. If possible, sit in the child's place, so that you have to guess as well!

Respond to the images, helping the children to be fully conscious of their beauty:

Teacher: *Isn't it interesting? What an amazing shape! How beautiful it is!*

2 Experiment by slowly turning an object, for example, a key, so that it becomes easier to identify.

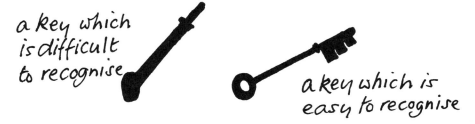

3 Now arrange some of the objects together to make an animal, and ask the children what they think it is.

Teacher: *What is it, do you think?*
Children: *It's a dog/cat/pig/horse,* etc.
Teacher: *It's a funny horse, isn't it? What is its head?*
Children: *Its head is a box.*
Teacher: *What are its legs?*
Children: *Its legs are pencils.*

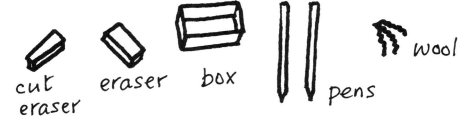

4 The class can now make an animal with you. The children can suggest various objects from their bags and pockets, which can be used to make the animal.

Child: *This is its head.*
Child: *This is its body.*
etc.

Make the animal first, and *then* decide what it is. The children might prefer to invent a name for the animal.

5 Put various thin cardboard (or paper) sheets with different holes cut in them on the screen. Here are some examples:

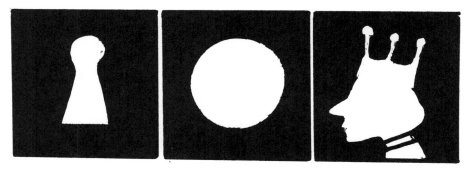

Give out a small piece of transparency and an overhead projector pen to each child. Ask them to draw anything they want. Project each piece of transparency, one at a time.

What can you see through the key hole?

What can you see through the telescope?

What can you see in the queen's head?

Ask the other children to suggest what the drawings might be, or what they can imagine seeing through the holes:

What is it/are they?
Where are they?
What time is it?
What is the weather like?
What are they doing?
What are they going to do next?
Why are they … ing?
etc.

6 Tell the children you would like them to make some pictures for a story. Remind them of the story *The Hare and the Tortoise* (or any other very short story). Here is a simple version of *The Hare and the Tortoise*, divided into scenes.

Scene 1
The hare says, 'I am a good runner! I am the best runner! Look!'
And Hare runs very quickly in a circle.
The other animals say, 'Oh, Hare! Shut up!'
The hare says, 'But I am the best!'

Scene 2
The tortoise says, 'Oh, Hare! Shut up! I am the best!
'You, the best?' laughs Hare.
'Yes, let's race!' says Tortoise.
'Race?' says Hare. 'That's silly! I am the best runner!'
'Let's start now!' says Tortoise. 'Let's go to the big tree!'

Scene 3
The hare talks to his friends, and he laughs and they laugh!
The tortoise walks.

Scene 4
The hare runs and he runs past the tortoise. 'You silly animal!'
he calls.
The tortoise says nothing. He walks.

Scene 5
The hare stops, lies down, and sleeps.
The tortoise walks past the hare.

Scene 6
The hare wakes up! 'Where's Tortoise? Oh, no!'
The tortoise is near the big tree! Hare jumps up and runs. And he
runs and runs, very fast.

Scene 7
The tortoise walks to the big tree. He is first!
All the animals laugh and shout and clap! 'Good old Tortoise!'
they shout.
The hare arrives! All the animals shout, 'Tortoise is the winner!'

Photocopiable © Oxford University Press

By questioning, get the children to say what animals and objects
they will need to tell the story. Basically: any animals, a hare, a
tortoise, a hill, a big tree, and perhaps the sun.

The images can be created in various ways: they can be drawn
with OHP pens, or cut out as silhouettes from thin card. You can
use real objects, for example, toy animals, or whatever materials
you have brought in. You might like to experiment with a
combination of these techniques.

The important thing is to continually encourage the children to
project what they are using, because what matters is if its shape
and texture are effective when projected. There is no point in a

child becoming attached to his or her object, and then finding it doesn't project very well.

7 Tell the story. Ask some of the children to move the pictures at the appropriate moments.

Tell the story a second time, and get the class to make sound effects: the tortoise gasping; the hare snoring, etc. and to add chanting representing: the hare, tortoise, other animals, trees, etc.

Examples of children chanting together:

Hare: *This is easy and I'm sleepy! This is easy and I'm sleepy!*
Tortoise: *Come on! Come on! Come on!*
Trees: *The hare is sleeping! The hare is sleeping! Silly, silly, silly Hare!*

8 Let the children, in groups, take over the performance. It might help to specify performance roles in each group:

Director. Narrator. Actors' voices. Puppet manipulators. Scene changers. Sound effects and chants.

VARIATION 1

Arrange objects on the screen so that they look visually satisfying. Don't expect to get too much language work out of it, but let the children experience its beauty. It is important for them to relax and to just enjoy the beauty! Experiment by projecting the image onto the ceiling, at an angle onto the wall, or onto children wearing white blouses or shirts.

VARIATION 2

With the children's help, arrange various objects to make a balanced-looking picture. If possible, choose some objects which have textured edges or holes in them, or are translucent. The children can call out, for example:

Put the comb in the middle/at the top/on the right, etc.!
That's nice/beautiful/interesting/boring/not very nice/not balanced!

FOLLOW-UP

The children can put on a show for other classes, or for a parents' evening. Working in groups, they can make the illustrations, and decide how to re-tell a story they know: any of the fables, for example, or a simplified version of a fairy story, or a local legend. They could also produce an illustrated book of the story, and a programme for the show.

Notes: Here are some other techniques you can use with the OHP:

1 Put various natural objects on the screen, for example, grass, flowers, a feather, water in a tightly-closed glass bottle (be careful with water near electricity, or a very hot lamp!).

2 Use a plastic transparency roll as a background, of the hillside, for example, then move it beneath the hare and the tortoise, to give the impression that they are moving.

3 Catch part of the projected image with a hand mirror, and project it onto the ceiling or any of the walls.

4 Put your head in profile on the OHP screen and have it massively projected—it will look like a giant's head! Eat things while your profile is being projected—this is very effective, and delights the children!

5 Put a piece of paper full of little holes of various sizes on the screen, covering it—this gives the effect of the night sky with stars and a moon.

6 Slowly move your hand or a book just under the reflector. This gives the effect of dawn and sunset.

7 Put coloured plastic on holes made in the images, e.g. for the fiery eyes of a dragon.

8 Move objects across the screen with a bit of 'Blu-tack' or putty pressed on them, and a straw or piece of wire pushed into it.

8.2 Shadow plays

Shadow plays are an ancient form of entertainment. The audience sits in front of a sheet suspended like a screen, and watch the shadows projected onto it. The shadows may be of real people and objects, or of puppets located behind the sheet which have a light source behind them. Most shadow plays tell a story.

The history of shadow plays

Shadow plays began in China 2,000 years ago. Then the idea spread to Indonesia and India, and from India to Egypt, Turkey, and Greece. This is the story of how the idea started:

Many years ago in China there was an Emperor. He was very sad because his wife had died. All day he sat in his room and cried. He didn't do his job at all, and everything went wrong. Now, there was an artist who lived in the palace. He saw that the Emperor was very unhappy, and he knew that the Emperor was not doing his job. He got an idea. He cut some card so that it looked like the Emperor's wife, and made it move behind a silk screen in the Emperor's room. He even imitated her voice! The Emperor was very happy, and he asked the artist to tell the story of his wife's life through the shadow theatre.

Children love creating characters, inventing situations, and performing for others to watch and listen. This medium is especially valuable for end-of-term shows. It will require a big effort on your part, but will be worth it in terms of the intense involvement of the children.

In the particular activity given here, the children concentrate on making puppets out of thin card. However, it is worth noting that the children themselves look wonderful in silhouette, as do other objects, such as house-plants, etc.

LEVEL	**All**
AGE	**4–12**
AIMS	**Language:** to improve fluency in speaking and listening. **Other:** making puppets; to learn to co-operate with others in putting on a performance.
TIME	As a broad guide, allow: **45 minutes to introduce the idea** **60 minutes to make the puppets** **45 minutes to make the story** **45 minutes to do rehearsals and so on** Life being what it is—add another hour!
MATERIALS	**For the lighting:** An overhead projector is the best source, as it provides a wide area of distributed light. Also, you can put things on the glass plate of the overhead projector and combine them with the puppets you hold against the screen. (See the illustration on the next page for more ways of using the overhead projector.) However, an ordinary table light works reasonably well, or even natural light from a window, particularly in the summer.

The audience sees silhouettes in black. Holes in the puppet show light and give variety.

Real leaves

Real person

Stick puppet

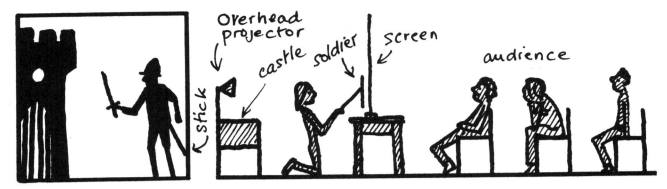

For the screen: a large white sheet such as a bedsheet, stretched tightly so that it is not crinkled. (See the illustration on this page for ways of making projection screens.) Or you can just use a single bright light in a darkened room, and cast the shadows on the walls and ceiling.

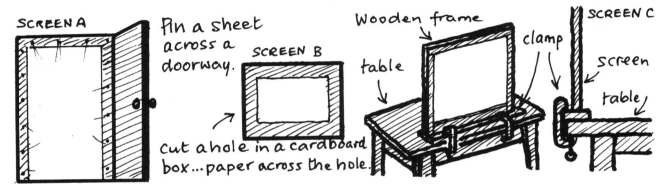

For the puppets: a copy of Worksheets 8.2A and B (pages 158–9) for each group; stiff paper or card, scissors, glue, sticky tape; thin canes, sticks, or thick wires to hold and to move the puppets. For you: a craft knife.

If you have a video camera, the children will love it if you record what they do, including the experiments and rehearsals.

You may like to add a musical background to the play. Even the simplest of musical instruments are enriching: stones in a plastic bottle, tambourines, recorders. Alternatively, you could use some recorded music.

PREPARATION

Make six basic puppets in order to let the children begin to experience shadow puppets immediately. Worksheets 8.2A and B explain everything. We suggest that you include a king and/or a queen, a prince and/or a princess, a monster, a bad person, and an animal. The puppets should be about 20 cm to 30 cm tall.

Note:

1 Most cards appear as a black silhouette, whatever colour they are.

2 Holes in a puppet will appear as white or as coloured if you stick coloured cellophane over the hole.

3 If you make a puppet out of white card, colour it, and then soak it in cooking oil, it will become translucent, and the colours will be very beautiful.

IN CLASS

1 Let the children play with making the shadows. Encourage them to find techniques you might not have thought of! Use English in identifying what it is they are representing. They can try putting their puppets, real objects, or their faces in profile against the screen and their hands on the overhead projector screen.

Who's this? What's this? What's he/she doing? These are very reasonable questions when mysterious shadows are seen.

The children will be very excited at first. Don't try to discourage this too much—it's an essential part of their creativity!

Help the children to appreciate that their image is usually best if they stand in profile or directly facing the screen rather than at an angle to it.

2 Brainstorm at least ten words for actions which the children might represent on the screen and write them on the board. The children take it in turns to choose one of the actions and mime it so that the class can identify the action.

3 Working in groups of two or three, the children choose a key moment from a story well-known to the class, rehearse it and then take it in turns to play their 'moment' behind the screen. The class try to identify what the performing group have played. Here are some key moments from two well-known stories:

Little Red Riding Hood
– Little Red Riding Hood talking to the wolf in the forest
– Little Red Riding Hood talking to the wolf who is lying in bed (on a table behind the screen)

The Frog Prince
– The princess kissing the frog (the frog could be a child with a jacket over his/her head!)

4 Put the children into groups of five or six. Hand out copies of Worksheets 8.2A and B, which give ideas for making puppets. While the designs given provide a starting point, they are not

meant to be copied exactly. Each group should make the following card puppets as a minimum:

- a prince or princess
- a king or queen
- a monster
- an interior, for example, a palace with a throne
- an exterior, for example, a wood

These represent fundamental characters and locations which almost automatically produce dramatic tensions, interactions, and good stories.

Emphasize that the outside shape of the puppets must be characterful, and that textures and decorative shapes all help to make the puppet look interesting. You can assist by cutting out eyes, decorative holes, fringes of hair, etc. with your craft knife.

During this 'making stage', give encouragement and advice. The children can also make comments.

I like it. That's good.
Give him a longer nose/long hair.
Cut out her eyes. Let me help you.
Please cut the holes.
Can I have the needle and cotton?

5 Encourage the children to experiment with the opportunities and challenges of using their puppets. First, let each group move their puppets about, just to get used to doing it. Then ask four children at a time to move their puppets to the sound of different kinds of music. (The children can make the music themselves, with different kinds of percussion instruments.) Ask two children at a time to try to move their figures to meet each other and talk, and then to go past each other to the other side of the screen.

6 Give advice and praise:

That's nice/wonderful/beautiful!
Keep the puppet flat on the screen!
Move the puppets slowly!
Speak clearly!

7 Groups of up to six children then work out some short scenes, which unless they want to add words, can be played in silence. For example:

- two or three of the puppets greet each other
- one puppet is angry with another puppet
- some terrible weather, for example, heavy rain, and what the characters do (and say)
- two puppets discuss an accident or disaster that happened the day before (past-tense forms)
- a puppet hears a frightening noise, hides, witnesses a horrible monster doing horrible things, then tells the story afterwards.

8 Depending on the age and proficiency of the children, either make up a story with the whole class, or ask each group to invent a story with the characters they have got.

If you decide to make the puppets and play with them as a whole class, the main challenge is to give each child something interesting to do!

- You might like to make use of the question-and-answer way of building up a story (described in detail in *Creating Stories with Children*, in this series). Basically, you ask questions to establish who is the main character in the story, where they are, what they are doing, and what happens next. This will involve the whole class. Of course, you can take an existing story and use the question-and-answer technique to recall and re-tell the story.
- Have some crowd scenes, lots of animals, and quite a lot of scenery, for example, trees, so that each child has something to make.
- In the performance, there can be several different scenes enabling the children manipulating the puppets to change.
- Sound effects can also be created by all the children not actually performing, for example, wind, rain, running feet, howling wolves, or the chanting of phrases.

9 Performance: Each group takes it in turn to rehearse and then perform their final production.

If you are working as a class, you can be the narrator, and tell or retell the story the first time, as the children take it in turns to operate the puppets, change the scenery, or make the sound effects. Later, a child can take on the narrator's role.

FOLLOW-UP 1   The children could put on a performance for another class, or for a 'parents and teachers' evening.

FOLLOW-UP 2   Make a video of the performances and play it back to the children.

FOLLOW-UP 3   Help them to make a book of the story or stories.

8.3 Making a video

In this activity, the children make, or pretend to make, a video, depending on whether or not you have access to a camera.

Children spend a large proportion of their time watching videos, so it is enriching for them to have some idea of how to make one. Furthermore, there is a real role for language use in the making of the video, as well as in the script itself.

In this particular activity, the children make a video based on their drawings, constructions, and models rather than on themselves as actors.

assistant   director   camera person   actors

LEVEL	**Elementary and above**

AGE

5–12. With the younger ones you would have to play a central role, but from the age of ten or eleven the children can organize themselves in production teams.

Only use the idea of making a storyboard from the age of about ten.

AIMS

Language: to improve speaking fluency.
Depending on the teaching policy, elementary-level children can restrict their use of English to the spoken parts of the characters and narrator, and learn the words orally, rather than from the written text.
Lower-intermediate level children can make use of their English in the making of the video.
Other: Acting; to learn how videos are made.

TIME

At least 4–5 hours

MATERIALS

One video camera, tripod, and video cassette for 15 children. Make sure that you can link it to a television with playback facilities. (Absolutely no expertise in using a video camera is required—though if you have any, it will be a bonus!)

Photocopies of:

– Worksheets 8.3A (page 160), illustrating good and bad shots and: *pan, tilt, zoom, close up, middle close up, long shot.*
– Worksheet 8.3B (page 161), illustrating a video storyboard (first page only),
– Worksheet 8.3C (page 162) giving examples of the Pied Piper puppet, adults, children, rats, houses, river, landscape.

Note:
It is not essential for the children to make a shooting script, but if they do, they should make a copy for each child in the group.

Sheets of A5 paper cut into viewfinders, or pretend cameras, as in the illustration on the next page.

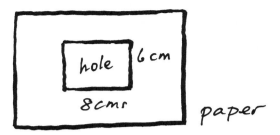

A tape recording of flute playing (or a child who can play the recorder).

Sticks, sticky paper, scissors.

IN CLASS

1 Play with the paper cameras and introduce the words *pan, zoom in, zoom out, close up, middle close up, long shot.*

2 Let the children experiment with the camera: panning, tilting, and zooming. Also let them play about in front of the camera. Encourage experimentation, for example, by coming right up to the lens to see what happens. Contrast slow pans and fast pans.

3 Show the Pied Piper of Hamelin puppet (see Worksheet 8.3C) on his stick. Invite the children to use their paper cameras on him, zooming in and out.

Establish who he is, and list all the words the children know from the story, e.g. *rat, town, river, money, children, mountain.* Teach the children the key words they don't know, for example, *He plays the pipe beautifully.*

4 Now tell the story fully in English. Move the puppet of the Pied Piper about, and mime as well as you can. Ask the children to continue the story, add a new ending to it (if necessary, in the mother tongue), and then put the chosen ending back into English.

The version of the story below is reduced to its simplest form. If your children are of a higher proficiency level, enrich the language accordingly.

Invite the children to add information. For example, in saying where the rats are in the town, and what they are like—*fat, thin, big, small, white, black, brown, ugly, beautiful*—and what they are doing in each of the places. This provides an opportunity for introducing some amusing scenes.

Note:

The use of the present tense in the text below is reasonable if associated with puppets actually moving about.

THE PIED PIPER OF HAMELIN

Scene 1

There is a town. Its name is Hamelin. It is in Germany.

There are a lot of rats in the town. The rats are in the houses, in the shops, in the parks, everywhere.

A man comes to the town. He says, 'I can take the rats away. Give me a lot of money!'

The people in the town say, 'First take the rats away, and then you get the money!'

The man plays his pipe beautifully. The rats listen. The rats come to him. The rats follow him.

Scene 2

The rats follow him to the river, and drown.

The man asks for money.

The people don't give him money.

Scene 3

The man plays his pipe beautifully, and all the children listen. The children come to him. The children follow him.

Scene 4

He walks to the mountain. The children walk to the mountain.

He walks into the mountain. The children walk into the mountain.

The people in the town are very sad. There are no children.

Scene 5

Your children's own ending!

---

5 List with the children what they will need for the story: rats, people, children, houses, river, mountain.

6 Give out the thin card, and agree with each child what he or she will make. We suggest that you tell the children what height to make the different characters or items, as follows:

   – grown-ups about 20 to 25 cm
   – children about 6 to 10 cm
   – rats about 3 to 5 cm
   – houses about 25 to 30 cm
   – mountain about 40 cm

You might decide that the children would benefit from having a copy of Worksheet 8.3C, giving ideas on puppets and on how to arrange the scenery.

While the children are making their puppets and scenery, give them every opportunity to see their work through the camera, or at least through their own paper cameras.

7 Divide the story into shooting scenes. I suggest using the scenes shown in the text above, and trying to record as many complete and presentable scenes as possible, to avoid time-consuming cutting.

8 Now the children make the video. Let them operate the puppets, speak the parts, make the music, operate the camera.

9 Play back their work, and let them enjoy watching it. If they want to, let them re-shoot the whole story with improvements.

VARIATIONS

There are other practical ways of making videos with children. I recommend that you consider the following:

Videos with costume, masks, and make-up.
Videos with more sophisticated puppets.
Real-life videos: documentaries, interviews, etc.

FOLLOW-UP

If the children (and you!) become familiar with making videos in the classroom, you will find it a great asset. As well as providing interesting and impressive entertainment for their parents, it provides the children with tremendous motivation to speak clearly and expressively, and to extend their vocabulary!

Appendix:
Materials and techniques

The main purpose of this Appendix is to provide teachers who are not art and crafts specialists with basic information about materials and techniques which you might find useful.

Paper

Paper sizes used in this book are based on the International Paper Sizes.

A0 is 841 x 1189 mm
A1 is 594 x 841 mm
A2 is 420 x 594 mm
A3 is 297 x 420 mm
A4 is 210 x 297 mm (the one we usually use for typing and letters, etc.)
A5 is 148 x 210 mm (the one we get when we fold A4 in half)
A6 is 105 x 148 mm
A7 is 74 x 105 mm

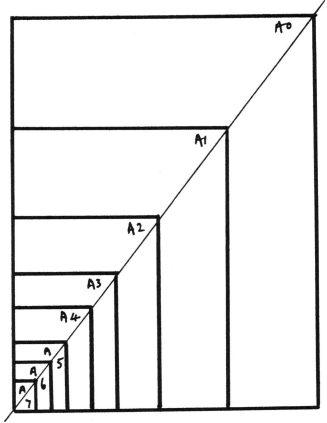

Variety of paper

It is exciting for children to paint and draw on different colours and textures of paper and, indeed, other material from cotton to wood and stone.

Furthermore, it is stimulating for the children to be given, or to create, sizes of paper which are not the International Paper Size.

A4 is such a conventional size in many Western countries that it has become boring … lacking in freshness … it is no longer stimulating in itself, either for the child in the act of creation or for the viewer of the work on display. The illustration shows some suggestions for overcoming this.

The largest piece of paper you can make up by taping together several very large sheets of paper.

Free paper or cheap paper

One source of free paper is a local printing works or newspaper, where thousands of 'off-cuts' may be thrown away every day. It is very common to find bins filled with paper and card measuring about 25 by 3 cm!

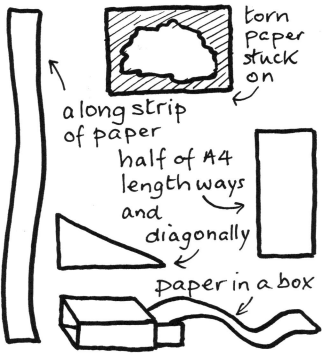

torn paper stuck on

a long strip of paper

half of A4 lengthways and diagonally

paper in a box

You can also use:

Wallpaper or (if it's widely available in your country) wallpaper lining paper
Used envelopes, opened out
Old wrapping paper
Boxes cut up
Sugar paper
The ends of rolls of paper from your local newspaper printing house.

Papier mâché

Tear newspapers into bits and mix with wallpaper paste. (This may contain a fungicide which might affect the skin of some children: if in doubt, use flour paste.) Make thin layers on a support of either wire mesh or clay. Soap the clay, or it will stick.

Papier mâché is very strong and light, and can be painted, but it takes a long time to dry—if you make it on a Friday, it might be dry by Monday.

It is good for making puppets and masks, giant figures of people or animals, and even small-scale scenery.

You can combine it with collage by sticking on objects, e.g. card rolls, plastic bottles, wood chippings, wire wool, etc.

But take into account that papier mâché is time-consuming to make and to dry … it can often be faster and easier to make masks and puppets with objects that you can stick and staple together. You can also use plaster and bandages.

Cardboard rolls

Cardboard rolls are always useful. Keep a box of them. They are often found in office dustbins.

A box of rubbish

Cardboard boxes, plastic bottles, and almost anything else which is not actually dangerous to the children is of huge potential for art and craft work with children. You can ask parents to bring clean boxes, etc. It isn't only that it saves money, but that the children are encouraged to see that even rubbish has value. It also helps them to think metaphorically—to see one thing as another—and to appreciate that, even with minimal resources, interesting and beautiful things can be made.

Knives and scissors

Scissors should have rounded ends—and should cut really well! Using scissors is a useful skill to learn. Cheap scissors often make a child's introduction to cutting very difficult indeed, while craft knives can be so useful—but dangerous! You should have one with a retractable blade for yourself, since you can then cut long lengths very quickly, and curves, and holes in the middle of a bit of card, which you can't do with scissors. Make sure you have a special surface which you always use when cutting things with a craft knife, to avoid damage to tables.

Paints, inks, pens, and brushes, etc.

Pens

Water-based pens are the most practical pens for children.

Alcohol-based pens are nice and bright but they might be permanent, and mark things you don't want marked. They could also stain through the paper the child is using.

Paints

Powder colour paints can be thickened with wallpaper paste or flour paste, and should be used in thick, cream-like mixtures. It is probably better to use these (and liquid poster paints) in the art room.

Tempera palettes of colour can be used thick or thin.

Water-colour paint can be used more thinly.

Brushes

Big, thick, and stiff hog-hair brushes are good for thick paint and a broad style. Have a wide range of brushes available, if possible. Teach children from the beginning never, never to stab brushes down so that the hair is forced sideways. Show pain if they do this and say *Poor brush! It's your friend. Don't stab it like that!*

Show the children how to control the water content of the brush by pulling it up and across the rim of the water pot.

Show children how important it is to wash the brushes between dipping them into different colours, so that the colours don't become muddy. And get them to clean the brushes when they have finished!

Crayons

These should be thick, especially those used by little children. Even older children get upset when their crayons break easily.

Oil pastels

These give rich colours.

Painting on plastic

To do this, add 1 teaspoonful of dishwashing liquid to half a cup of thick liquid paint.

Glue and staples

Put old newspapers over the table top when gluing. Put the glue or paste in large pots, in small quantities. Put in a cooking spatula or a long piece of wood to reduce the chance of getting glue on your fingers.

PVA (polyvinyl acetate) is the best glue for most purposes. It dries transparent. It should be washed out of clothing immediately, but in general is not damaging or dangerous. It can be used for wood or paper.

Wallpaper paste (if you can get it in your country) is cheap, and lasts for several days if kept covered. However, it may contain a fungicide which might affect the skin of some children: if this is a problem, use flour paste, which is a very practical kind of paste to make and keep in schools. To make flour paste: add a cup of flour to three-quarters of a cup of cold water, stirring as you do so. This makes a thin mixture. Heat this mixture slowly up to boiling, still stirring. Boil until you have a thick consistency. Continue to stir all the time. If you want to keep the paste add a few drops of oil of cloves or peppermint as a preservative. Thin it with cold water. Keep the paste in the fridge.

For metal and fabrics: read the labels on tubes of glue, and see what they claim to stick. Note that plastic containers, round objects such as cardboard rolls, and very shiny non-absorbent surfaces, don't glue easily. Use staples to add strength.

Sticky tape: It is best to keep the tape on a dispenser, because in that way you don't have to search for the end. However, if you have no dispenser it helps to drag your finger across the sticky side at the end before you put the tape down. In this way you can easily find the end the next time you need it.

Mounted on coloured or black paper.
Different shapes given 'discipline by lining up the top edges.

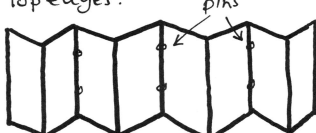

Zigzag folds pinned to the the wall or standing on a table.

← Large or long pictures pinned top and bottom to pieces of wood.

Pictures displayed in a box. Peep through the hole!

Displays and exhibitions

Exhibitions are important for encouraging responsibility and concern for others.

Let the children take part in the planning of the exhibition so that they have to think about how they can help other people to see and enjoy their work.

Exhibitions are also important because the children want their work to be good enough, and this makes them willing to work even harder!

Places for exhibitions: classroom, head teacher's office, local bank, local bookshop, library, café, art gallery, the British Embassy, etc.

A few practical tips:

1 Mount the work on coloured or black paper, with a narrow margin around the picture to act as a frame.

2 The work should either be arranged in very straight lines, or have a clearly asymmetrical shape.

3 Big pictures can be pinned on the upper and lower edges to pieces of wood measuring about 50 mm x 300 mm. This will keep the paper tight, and the upper strip of wood can be fastened to or hung from the wall.

4 Titles and captions can be informative, provocative, expressive, clear, ambiguous or questioning, depending on their purpose.

5 Look for opportunities to include three-dimensional displays. For example, if you fold paper in a concertina and pin it on the creases, you will create a three-dimensional (3-D) ripple effect. You could also consider hanging banners or 3-D spy boxes.

Clay, plasticine, modelling clay, 'playdough'

Clay has been used for modelling since Palaeolithic times. It is a fundamental substance. Making images from material taken out of the ground is an extremely important activity for children to experience. Furthermore, it makes the child think in three dimensions, in a world where so much is two-dimensional or simulated 3-D, but is actually seen on a flat screen. In this age of virtual reality (which is actually total deception), the experience of making things with clay becomes particularly important.

Clay which has been prepared for sale to potters is cheap. Phone a local art school or secondary school and ask the pottery teacher where the nearest source is. Clay has great character. It is messy, but not too difficult to clean—water and a cloth will be all you need. If you leave it exposed to the air it will dry out in a few hours or days, but if you spray it with water and store it in a tightly-packed plastic bag it will stay moist for a few months. Dried-out clay can be recycled by putting it in a plastic bucket with 2 or 3 cm of water in the bottom, and a lid or plastic cover fastened round with an elastic band. After a day or two, put the wet clay onto a wooden board and knead it again. However, children must not do this, and adults should always wear a cloth face mask, to prevent the clay dust entering their lungs.

If cracks appear during modelling, they can be repaired by pressing-in more clay, or by sponging it with a damp sponge.

Unfinished work should be covered with a wet cloth, or wet paper towels with plastic on top. Ideally, you should store these half-finished pieces in a cupboard.

Clay can be painted as soon as it has been modelled, or later, when dry.

Half-dry clay can be carved. If left to harden, unless it is dropped, clay will last for years. It can also be fired in a kiln. Clay dust is harmful to health, so once dry, it should not be sand-papered without special precautions being taken. Some people think clay must be dirty because it comes from the ground, but it is actually a very clean medium.

Use a board made of wood or cardboard, as a working surface. While heavy plastic may also be used, clay may stick to it, so you have to wash the surface after use.

Playdough and Saltdough

You can buy ready-prepared 'playdough' in toyshops, or make it yourself. Alternatively, you (and the children) can also make playdough and saltdough. The children can make similar things with both types of material, but it's worth knowing that, once cooked, playdough is tougher, and is easier to play with.

Playdough

For each child, you need:

100 grams of plain flour
50 grams of salt
1 teaspoonful of cream of tartar
1 tablespoonful of oil
150 milligrams of water

Technique 1

1 Put everything except the water in a big pan.

2 Add the water slowly and mix.

3 Put the pan over a medium heat, and stir constantly.

4 Continue to stir until the dough is very stiff.

5 Take out the dough and put it onto a smooth surface.

6 Wash the pan immediately.

Technique 2

1 Mix the ingredients in a large microwave bowl.

2 Put the bowl in the microwave, and cook at full power for one minute.

3 Remove the bowl from the microwave, and stir the dough.

4 Cook again for about 2 minutes, until the dough begins to pull away from the side of the bowl, and becomes very stiff. Stir once or twice during this second cooking.

5 Put the dough onto a smooth surface, and knead it.

Colour playdough

Colour playdough with food colouring when you mix the ingredients, or paint on the finished objects.

Storing playdough

Keep playdough in a plastic bag, inside a plastic container.

Saltdough

Saltdough is easier to prepare than playdough. For each child, you will need:

100 grams of plain flour
100 grams of salt (fine)
1/3 of a tablespoon of oil
100 milligrams of water

Technique

1 Mix the ingredients in a large bowl.

2 Put the dough onto a floured smooth surface. Knead the dough until it is smooth and elastic.

Modelling the dough

I recommend that you teach these basic skills the first time that children—particularly the very young ones—experience saltdough.

Flat sheets: roll with a bottle or drinking glass.

Sausages for legs, etc.: roll them to and fro across a flat surface with your hands.

Balls: roll them round and round on a flat surface with the palm.

Domes: roll a ball and cut it in half.

Joining dough

To join two pieces: scratch and wet the surfaces to be joined.

The surface of the dough can be marked with any type of sharp object: ends of spoons for smiles, pencil ends and sides, forks, coins, etc.

Colouring the dough

You can add food colour at any stage before baking.

You can paint the dough after it has been baked, using water-based paints and felt pens.

Baking the dough

Small objects need 10 to 20 minutes on a lightly oiled baking tray at gas mark 4 (about 180 Centigrade).

Printing

Printing is a key experience for all children—the idea of making multiple copies is exciting. Encourage them to think of the invention of printing texts, and all of its effects!

There are various ways of printing, but with children it is best to use protruding surfaces. Rather than cut the shapes, which is difficult, children should experiment with shapes cut specially by you, or with objects such as bottle tops, corks, polystyrene, vegetables (potato, carrot, cabbage) junk, toys, building blocks, etc. (see chapter 3).

Here are some hints:

- Use thick liquid paint. Keep some in a plastic container with a sponge. If possible, use deep containers to minimise drip.
- Aim for the build-up of patterns or pictures.
- Aim for accuracy but also for a sense of repetition and pattern.
- Apply the paint by pressing the printing surface to the paint or by using a roller.

Reducing the mess

Most of the activities given in this book do not create mess. However, tidying up offers an authentic opportunity—not to be missed by the language teacher!—to use language with meaning and purpose.

Paints and clay can be messy, so children should wear overalls or pinafores. Cover the desks with plastic sheets or old newspapers.

Further reading

Many of the activities in the books in the Oxford University Press Resource Books for Teachers (see page 143) for young learners are essentially based on art and crafts.

The best publisher for practical books on art and craft is Usborne Books, which can be found in translation in almost every country in the world.

Gibson. R. 1992. *Make and Play*. London: Usborne Books.

See also **Wright A.** *1000 + Pictures for Teachers to Copy*, (Longman).

This book offers you and the children a vast number of simple representations of people, animals, objects, and scenes to copy. However, there is a danger that too much copying of such pictures might rob the children of their own freshness of vision.

Other titles in the Resource Books for Teachers series

Beginners by Peter Grundy – Communicative activities for both absolute and 'false' beginners, including those who do not know the Roman alphabet. All ages. (ISBN 0 19 437200 6)

Class Readers by Jean Greenwood – Activities to develop extensive and intensive reading skills, plus listening and speaking tasks. All ages. (ISBN 0 19 437103 4)

Classroom Dynamics by Jill Hadfield – Helps teachers maintain a good working relationship with their classes, and so promote effective learning. Teenagers and adults. (ISBN 0 19 437147 6)

Conversation by Rob Nolasco and Lois Arthur – Over 80 activities to develop students' ability to speak confidently and fluently. Teenagers and adults. (ISBN 0 19 437096 8)

Creating Stories with Children by Andrew Wright – Encourages creativity, confidence, and fluency and accuracy in spoken and written English. Age 7–14. (ISBN 0 19 437204 9)

Cultural Awareness by Barry Tomalin and Susan Stempleski – Challenges stereotypes, using cultural issues as a rich resource for language practice. Teenagers and adults. (ISBN 0 19 437194 8)

Dictionaries by Jonathan Wright – Ideas for making more effective use of dictionaries in class. Teenagers and adults. (ISBN 0 19 437219 7)

Drama by Charlyn Wessels – Creative and enjoyable activities using drama to teach spoken communication skills and literature. Teenagers and adults. (ISBN 0 19 437097 6)

Drama with Children by Sarah Phillips – Practical ideas to develop speaking skills, self-confidence, imagination, and creativity. Age 6–12. (ISBN 0 19 437220 0)

Exam Classes by Peter May – Preparation for a wide variety of public examinations, including most of the main American and British exams. Teenagers and adults. (ISBN 0 19 437208 1)

Games for Children by Gordon Lewis with Günther Bedson – An exciting collection of games for children aged 4 to 12. (ISBN 0 19 437224 3)

Grammar Dictation by Ruth Wajnryb – The 'dictogloss' technique – improves understanding and use of grammar by reconstructing texts. Teenagers and adults. (ISBN 0 19 437004 6)

The Internet by Scott Windeatt, David Hardisty, and David Eastment – Motivates learners and brings a wealth of material into the classroom. For all levels of expertise. Teenagers and adults. (ISBN 0 19 437223 5)

Learner-based Teaching by Colin Campbell and Hanna Kryszewska – Unlocks the wealth of knowledge that learners bring to the classroom. All ages. (ISBN 0 19 437163 8)

Letters by Nicky Burbidge, Peta Gray, Sheila Levy, and Mario Rinvolucri – Using letters and e-mail for language and cultural study. Teenagers and adults. (ISBN 0 19 442149 X)

Listening by Goodith White – Advice and ideas for encouraging learners to become 'active listeners'. Teenagers and adults. (ISBN 0 19 437216 2)

Literature by Alan Maley and Alan Duff – An innovatory book on using literature for language practice. Teenagers and adults. (ISBN 0 19 437094 1)

Music and Song by Tim Murphey – 'Tuning in' to students' musical tastes can increase motivation and tap a rich vein of resources. All ages. (ISBN 0 19 437055 0)

Newspapers by Peter Grundy – Original ideas for making effective use of newspapers in lessons. Teenagers and adults. (ISBN 0 19 437192 6)

Projects with Young Learners by Diane Phillips, Sarah Burwood, and Helen Dunford – Encourages learner independence by producing a real sense of achievement. Age 5 to 13. (ISBN 0 19 437221 9)

Project Work by Diana L. Fried-Booth – Bridges the gap between the classroom and the outside world. Teenagers and adults. (ISBN 0 19 437092 5)

Pronunciation by Clement Laroy – Imaginative activities to build confidence and improve all aspects of pronunciation. All ages. (ISBN 0 19 437087 9)

Role Play by Gillian Porter Ladousse – Controlled conversations to improvised drama, simple dialogues to complex scenarios. Teenagers and adults. (ISBN 0 19 437095 X)

Self-Access by Susan Sheerin – Advice on setting up and managing self-access study facilities, plus materials. Teenagers and adults. (ISBN 0 19 437099 2)

Storytelling with Children by Andrew Wright – Hundreds of exciting ideas for using stories to teach English to children aged 7 to 14. (ISBN 0 19 437202 2)

Translation by Alan Duff – A wide variety of translation activities from many different subject areas. Teenagers and adults. (ISBN 0 19 437104 2)

Very Young Learners by Vanessa Reilly and Sheila M. Ward – Advice and ideas for teaching children aged 3 to 6 years, including games, songs, drama, stories, and art and crafts. (ISBN 0 19 437209 X)

Video by Richard Cooper, Mike Lavery, and Mario Rinvolucri – Original ideas for watching and making videos. All ages. (ISBN 0 19 437102 6)

Vocabulary by John Morgan and Mario Rinvolucri – A wide variety of communicative activities for teaching new words. Teenagers and adults. (ISBN 019 437091 7)

Writing by Tricia Hedge – A wide range of writing tasks, as well as guidance on student difficulties with writing. Teenagers and adults. (ISBN 0 19 437098 4)

Young Learners by Sarah Phillips – Advice and ideas for teaching English to children aged 6–12, including arts and crafts, games, stories, poems, and songs. (ISBN 0 19 437195 6)

toothpaste box

chimney

corrugated card

cover the walls with white or coloured paper

Cut off the shaded 10 cm

All the buildings based on cardboard boxes.

SUPERMARKET

cut windows and doors out of coloured paper and glue to the building

Cut small pictures of objects and food, etc from publicity adverts, etc. and glue onto the windows.

fold

bridge

fold

about 10 cm

Use card for the bridge. Pull it over the edge of a table and this will create the curve.

cut to open

Photocopiable © Oxford University Press

tree

card

plasticene

cow

Press the two pieces of paper together and cut them both at the same time.

traffic lights

card

plasticene

car

two boxes

card wheels

silver kitchen foil

pond

Photocopiable © Oxford University Press

plastic bowl

ball

pencil

roll

tissue paper

card for arms and legs

matchbox

paper

bottle

←straw

string →

sticks

Masks based on paper plates.

Fastened either with string/elastic, etc.
Or with paper strips.

←6→ 0cm 0

Cuts with a knife

The teacher makes all the eyes in the masks with a knife: criss cross cuts, then fold them back.

nose

mouth

The children can cut the features out of paper and stick them on or draw them.

corrugated card

wool

wire wool

hat added

cotton wool

cork

string

paper handkerchiefs

POLICE

plastic cup

yellow paper

Photocopiable © Oxford University Press

dog

owl

pig

staple

or glue

insect bug

teddy bear

red card

cat

elephant

sheep

spider

lion

cut the edges of the plate

head and ears a different piece of card

spring

frog

2 plates

folded plate

box

alien

alien

Photocopiable © Oxford University Press

Make a robot!

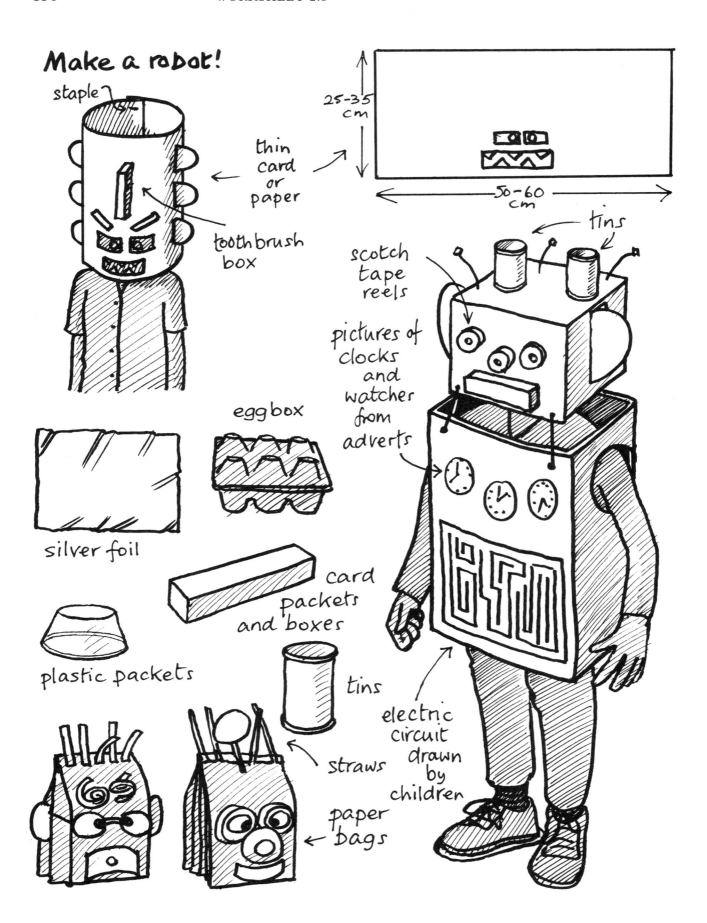

staple

thin card or paper

toothbrush box

25-35 cm

50-60 cm

tins

scotch tape reels

pictures of clocks and watches from adverts

silver foil

egg box

card packets and boxes

plastic packets

tins

straws

electric circuit drawn by children

paper bags

Photocopiable © Oxford University Press

The Sporse

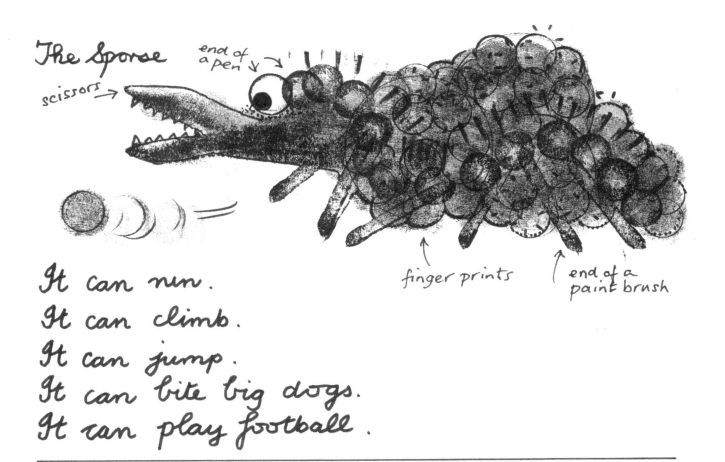

finger prints

end of a
paint brush

scissors

end of
a pen

It can run.
It can climb.
It can jump.
It can bite big dogs.
It can play football.

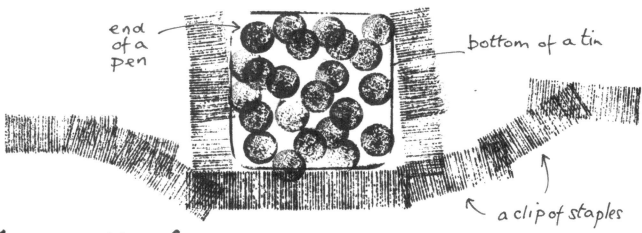

end
of a
Pen

bottom of a tin

a clip of staples

It can think.
It can speak in English.
It can sing.
It can laugh.
It can cry.

Photocopiable © Oxford University Press

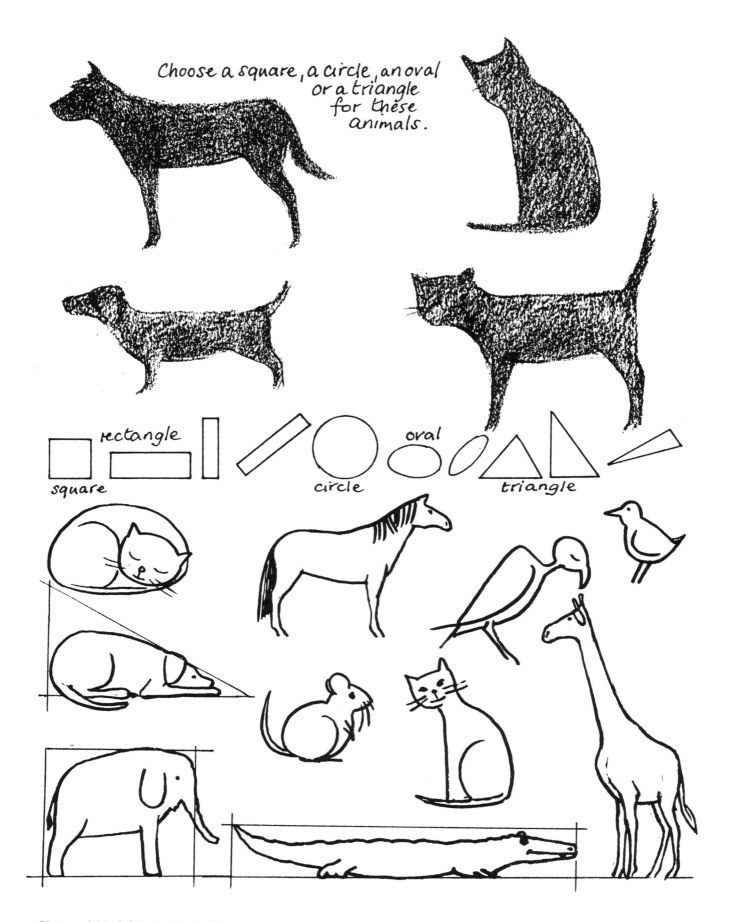

Choose a square, a circle, an oval or a triangle for these animals.

rectangle

square

circle

oval

triangle

Photocopiable © Oxford University Press

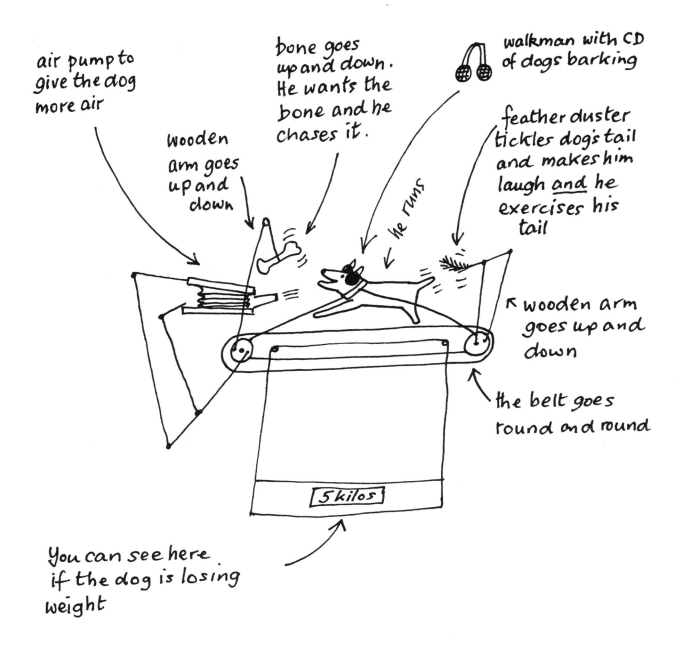

air pump to give the dog more air

Wooden arm goes up and down

bone goes up and down. He wants the bone and he chases it.

he runs

walkman with CD of dogs barking

feather duster tickles dog's tail and makes him laugh and he exercises his tail

wooden arm goes up and down

the belt goes round and round

5 kilos

You can see here if the dog is losing weight

When the dog is tired it walks and then stops. The belt goes slowly and then stops ... then the bone stops going up and down, the air pump stops, the feather duster stops tickling him. Then he can lie down and sleep.

Photocopiable © Oxford University Press

Photocopiable © Oxford University Press

Glue your shield onto coloured card then cut the card.

Cut your shield from A5 paper.

Different designs   Oxford University

Timi's coat of arms. She likes cats stories and birds.

Alexa's donkey coat of arms

school

for ghosts

for skateboarders

for nature

Photocopiable © Oxford University Press

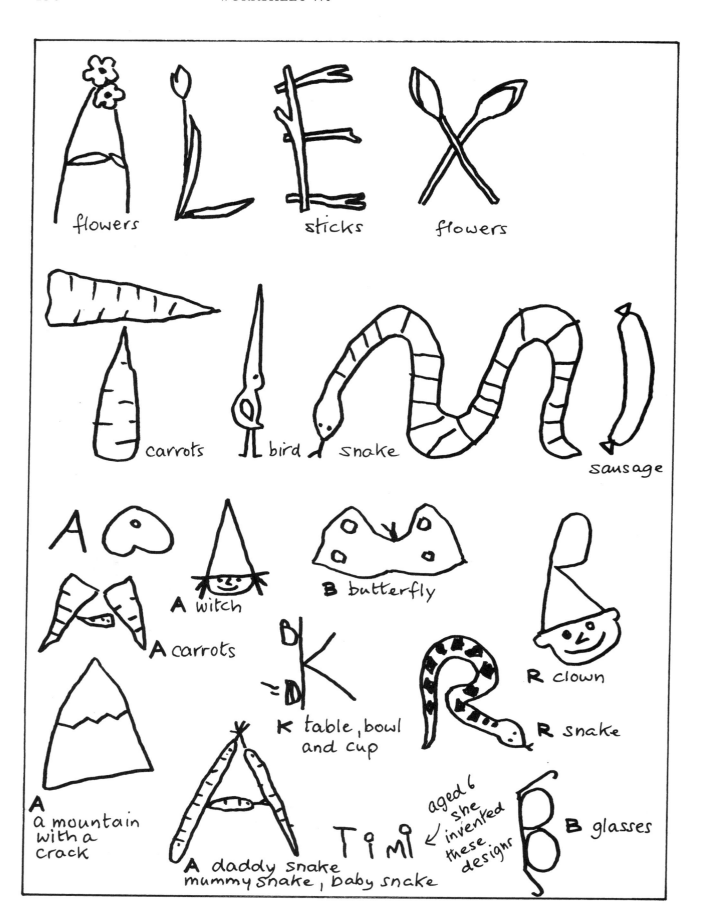

Photocopiable © Oxford University Press

In Whitby you can......

Photocopiable © Oxford University Press

How to make shadow puppets

thin card — interesting shape

boring shape →

1-2cm corrugated card on the back of the puppet

sticky tape

Push the paper clip in.

stick about 30cm

Colour the holes with coloured cellophane, etc.

Cut out holes with a knife

split pin

thread

stick to move the arm

Two ways of moving the arm: split pin or thread.

Cut the door and window then you can open and close them.

Photocopiable © Oxford University Press

one arm hinged

head hinged

lace

each part hinged

HAPPY CAT

END

cotton

The scenes (hills, castles, rooms, shops, etc.) can be put on the OHP or be made of card and put behind the screen.

Some papers are translucent

screen

card

table

The people must be about the right size for all scenes.

Photocopiable © Oxford University Press

Photocopiable © Oxford University Press

SPEAKING	SOUND	PICTURE
RATS: squeaking PEOPLE: shouting	Squeaks Shouts	 PAN RIGHT
MAN: There are rats in the houses! WOMAN: There are rats in the streets! MAN: What can we do?	Squeaks	 ZOOM TO FACES
PIPER: I can take the rats away. WOMAN: How much does it cost? PIPER: Less than a nightmare. MAN: First take the rats then we will give you the money.	Squeaks	 MCU
MAN: Look! The rats are going! They are following him!	Flute	 PAN RIGHT THEN LEFT TO PIED PIPER

Photocopiable © Oxford University Press

Photocopiable © Oxford University Press

Indexes

'v' refers to a Variation of an activity.
'f' refers to a Follow-up.